SLAYING TODAY'S GIANTS

BROTHER ANDREW
AND AL JANSSEN

Copyright © 2013 by Open Doors International

Published by Open Doors International
P.O. Box 27001
Santa Ana, CA 92799

www.OpenDoors.org

ISBN: 978-1-935701-03-3

Printed in the United States of America

Unless otherwise indicated, all Scripture quotations are from The Holy Bible, English Standard Version® (ESV®), copyright© 2001 by Crossway, a publishing ministry of Good News Publishing. Used by permission. All rights reserved.

Scripture taken from the Holy Bible, International Version®, NIV®. Copyright © 1973, 1978, 1984, 2011 by Biblica, Inc.™ Used by permission of Zondervan. All rights reserved worldwide. www.zondervan.com

The "NIV" and "New International Version" are trademarks registered in the United States Patent and Trademark Offices by Biblica, Inc.™

All rights reserved. No part of this publication may be reproduced, stored in a retrieval system, or transmitted in any form or by any means—electronic, mechanical, photocopying, recording, or otherwise—without prior written permission from Open Doors International.

Cover design by Dugan Design Group
Interior design and typeset Katherine Lloyd, The DESK

CONTENTS

INTRODUCTION 5

PART ONE - THE PROBLEM

1   THE WRONG PLACE AT THE WRONG TIME 15
2   IMPOSSIBLE ODDS 18
3   A MOST INTIMIDATING OPPONENT 21
4   A WAR OF WORDS 25
5   TOTAL BRAINWASHING 27
6   WHERE'S THE MAN? 31
7   WHO'S AFRAID OF THE BIG BAD GIANT? 34

PART TWO - INTRODUCING THE MAN OF GOD

8   WHERE DID HE COME FROM? 39
9   A VITAL COMPONENT 42
10   HOW TO PRAY FOR A FAILING LEADER 45
11   PREPARE TO BE GOD'S ANSWER 48
12   THE ANTIDOTE TO FEAR 51
13   FIRST IMPRESSIONS CAN BE WRONG 54
14   WHAT WAS JESSE THINKING? 58
15   EVERY SHEEP IS PRECIOUS 61
16   GOD'S CHOICE REVEALED 64
17   A LOOK UNDER THE HOOD 67
18   DAVID'S OPPORTUNITY IS KNOCKING 71

PART THREE - PREPARING FOR BATTLE

19 WHAT TO DO WITH THE WRONG MESSAGE 77
20 A CONFRONTATION PHILOSOPHY 80
21 RIGHT AND WRONG MOTIVES 83
22 WHY DAVID HAD TO RESPOND 86
23 FAMILY BACKLASH 89
24 GOD OPENS THE DOOR 92
25 A CRAZY IDEA 95
26 A FEEBLE ATTEMPT TO HELP GOD 98

PART FOUR - THE BATTLE

27 AN ARSENAL OF FIVE STONES 103
28 THE ENEMY SPEAKS 105
29 DAVID RESPONDS. 108
30 THE REASON FOR THE BATTLE 111
31 TO THE DEATH. 114
32 LESSONS FROM THE BATTLEFIELD 119
33 BACK WHERE THEY BELONG 122
34 IT'S NOT OVER YET. 125
35 WIN THE WAR. 128
36 THREE DOWN, TWO TO GO 131
37 AM I READY TO FIGHT?. 135
38 BACK TO THE FUTURE 138
     NOTES. 143

INTRODUCTION

We all know the story—David versus Goliath. We learned it in Sunday school and enjoyed hearing it read from picture storybooks. It's the inspirational metaphor for the underdog sports team facing an undefeated opponent. It's the motivation for a start-up company competing against a corporate giant.

So why revisit such a familiar drama? Because when we stop and look closely, there are some things about this story that are relevant to the spiritual warfare we experience today.

It's interesting how the two armies—Israel and the Philistines—are positioned for battle yet no one lifts a sword. Not a single spear is thrown. No one is killed. There is just a lot of trash talk! Sounds like a big football match or election coverage in the media today.

Here's the matchup. On one side stands a giant, a massive trained warrior. Undefeated, impregnable, overconfident, he issues the challenge: Send me your best man! We will fight. Loser serves the winner. No need for all of you to die in battle. Isn't it better for one man to die for all?

So reasonable, don't you think?

Meet our second contestant. No, not David. It's Saul, King Saul, tallest man in all Israel. A trained soldier, he is also undefeated! Saul versus Goliath. This is the match everyone expected, anticipated. Saul's entire life had prepared him for this defining moment.

So where was Saul? He was hiding in his tent. He had no intention of fighting the giant. (Neither did David. He came to the scene on an errand for his father, Jesse.) Saul knew he couldn't win. No doubt he prayed—for a savior. Anybody but him, he thought. He'd write a check for half his personal wealth to the one who killed the giant. He'd give his prettiest daughter in marriage to the champion. What other incentive could he provide? Okay, no taxes for the winner's entire family for life. Surely those were enough inducements to recruit a champion.

However, no one stepped forward—for forty days—until a teenage boy showed up.

So that's the situation. You know the ending. This story has been told and retold until there is no surprise left. Yet we should be surprised, amazed even, at what happened on that battlefield.

Let's take a closer look at David. Not the nine-foot-tall statue of him as carved in marble by Michelangelo. Let's remember, David was a boy—eighteen years old max! He didn't have any physical advantage. He wasn't rich. He didn't come from a prestigious family. He didn't graduate from a leading university. He had no unique talents—except that he was gifted musically, which doesn't exactly qualify you for officer training in any army.

Naturally, we admire David because he stood up to an unbeatable foe and won. The tragedy is that David should not have been unique. He only did what anyone in Israel could have done. Well, what anyone could have done if he or she had thought like David.

What made David so special? Not his cleverness or courage, though he surely had both. Rather, he was unique for one reason. The Bible says he was a man after God's heart (1 Samuel 13:14). Wow! How did David attain such divine approval? Can we have it too?

Maybe the example of David can impact our lives today. Just maybe he can show us how to confront, and defeat, the giants we face. Consider this: David saw what everyone saw. David heard what everyone heard. However, David thought what no one thought. As a result, David said what no one said and did what no one did.

It appears that David knew something no one else seemed to

INTRODUCTION

know. Ah, but *you* can know what David knew. *You* can do what David did. God wants to give you everything He provided David to defeat today's giants.

That's why Al and I believe the life of David remains so relevant today. Through him we learn to confront the fears—cultural, political, even religious—that intimidate so many Christians. Like Israel, we face giants. Your giants might be personal—a marital crisis, a rebellious child, the loss of a job, cancer. We face national and international giants like economic turmoil, political upheavals, and the spread of Islamic fundamentalism, not to mention terrorism. Are we going to cower in fear like Saul? Or will we step forward and trust God like the teenage shepherd?

Actually, most of us would rather be spectators than combatants. That's a big problem with Christians today. It's time to stand up, climb down the stadium steps, and step onto the arena. The choice is ours. If David had stayed on the sidelines, we wouldn't have this powerful story. If we remain seated in the stands, we will never know just how God desires to do something remarkable, miraculous even, through us. For this story isn't about an undersized hero. It's about the greatness of God and the spiritual war He's called each one of us to fight.

1 SAMUEL 17

Now the Philistines gathered their armies for battle. And they were gathered at Socoh, which belongs to Judah, and encamped between Socoh and Azekah, in Ephes-dammim. And Saul and the men of Israel were gathered, and encamped in the Valley of Elah, and drew up in line of battle against the Philistines. And the Philistines stood on the mountain on the one side, and Israel stood on the mountain on the other side, with a valley between them. And there came out from the camp of the

Philistines a champion named Goliath of Gath, whose height was six cubits and a span. He had a helmet of bronze on his head, and he was armed with a coat of mail, and the weight of the coat was five thousand shekels of bronze. And he had bronze armor on his legs, and a javelin of bronze slung between his shoulders. The shaft of his spear was like a weaver's beam, and his spear's head weighed six hundred shekels of iron. And his shield-bearer went before him. He stood and shouted to the ranks of Israel, "Why have you come out to draw up for battle? Am I not a Philistine, and are you not servants of Saul? Choose a man for yourselves, and let him come down to me. If he is able to fight with me and kill me, then we will be your servants. But if I prevail against him and kill him, then you shall be our servants and serve us." And the Philistine said, "I defy the ranks of Israel this day. Give me a man, that we may fight together." When Saul and all Israel heard these words of the Philistine, they were dismayed and greatly afraid.

Now David was the son of an Ephrathite of Bethlehem in Judah, named Jesse, who had eight sons. In the days of Saul the man was already old and advanced in years. The three oldest sons of Jesse had followed Saul to the battle. And the names of his three sons who went to the battle were Eliab the firstborn, and next to him Abinadab, and the third Shammah. David was the youngest. The three eldest followed Saul, but David went back and forth from Saul to feed his father's sheep at Bethlehem. For forty days the Philistine came forward and took his stand, morning and evening.

And Jesse said to David his son, "Take for your brothers an ephah of this parched grain, and these ten loaves, and carry them quickly to the camp to your brothers. Also take these ten cheeses to the commander of their thousand. See if your brothers are well, and bring some token from them."

Now Saul and they and all the men of Israel were in the Valley of Elah, fighting with the Philistines. And David rose early in the morning

INTRODUCTION

and left the sheep with a keeper and took the provisions and went, as Jesse had commanded him. And he came to the encampment as the host was going out to the battle line, shouting the war cry. And Israel and the Philistines drew up for battle, army against army. And David left the things in charge of the keeper of the baggage and ran to the ranks and went and greeted his brothers. As he talked with them, behold, the champion, the Philistine of Gath, Goliath by name, came up out of the ranks of the Philistines and spoke the same words as before. And David heard him.

All the men of Israel, when they saw the man, fled from him and were much afraid. And the men of Israel said, "Have you seen this man who has come up? Surely he has come up to defy Israel. And the king will enrich the man who kills him with great riches and will give him his daughter and make his father's house free in Israel." And David said to the men who stood by him, "What shall be done for the man who kills this Philistine and takes away the reproach from Israel? For who is this uncircumcised Philistine, that he should defy the armies of the living God?" And the people answered him in the same way, "So shall it be done to the man who kills him."

Now Eliab his eldest brother heard when he spoke to the men. And Eliab's anger was kindled against David, and he said, "Why have you come down? And with whom have you left those few sheep in the wilderness? I know your presumption and the evil of your heart, for you have come down to see the battle." And David said, "What have I done now? Was it not but a word?" And he turned away from him toward another, and spoke in the same way, and the people answered him again as before.

When the words that David spoke were heard, they repeated them before Saul, and he sent for him. And David said to Saul, "Let no man's heart fail because of him. Your servant will go and fight with this Philistine." And Saul said to David, "You are not able to go against this Philistine to fight with him, for you are but a youth, and he has been a man of war from his youth." But David said to Saul, *"Your servant used to keep sheep for his father. And when there came a lion, or a bear, and took a lamb from the flock, I went after him and struck him and delivered it out of his mouth. And if he arose against me, I caught him by his beard and struck him and killed him. Your servant has struck down both lions and bears, and this uncircumcised Philistine shall be like one of them, for he has defied the armies of the living God."* And David said, *"The* Lord *who delivered me from the paw of the lion and from the paw of the bear will deliver me from the hand of this Philistine."* And Saul said to David, *"Go, and the* Lord *be with you!"*

Then Saul clothed David with his armor. He put a helmet of bronze on his head and clothed him with a coat of mail, and David strapped his sword over his armor. And he tried in vain to go, for he had not tested them. Then David said to Saul, "I cannot go with these, for I have not tested them." So David put them off. Then he took his staff in his hand and chose five smooth stones from the brook and put them in his shepherd's pouch. His sling was in his hand, and he approached the Philistine.

And the Philistine moved forward and came near to David, with his shield-bearer in front of him. And when the Philistine looked and saw David, he disdained him, for he was but a youth, ruddy and handsome in appearance. And the Philistine said to David, "Am I a dog, that you come to me with sticks?" And the Philistine cursed David by his gods. The Philistine said to David, "Come to me, and I will give your flesh to the birds of the air and to the beasts of the field." Then David said to the Philistine, *"You come to me with a sword and with a spear and with a javelin, but I come to you in the name of the* Lord *of hosts, the God of the armies of Israel, whom you have defied. This day the* Lord *will deliver you into my hand, and I will strike you down and cut off your head. And I will give the dead bodies of the host of the Philistines this day to the birds of the air and to the wild beasts of the earth, that all the*

INTRODUCTION

earth may know that there is a God in Israel, and that all this assembly may know that the Lord *saves not with sword and spear. For the battle is the* Lord's, *and he will give you into our hand."*

When the Philistine arose and came and drew near to meet David, David ran quickly toward the battle line to meet the Philistine. And David put his hand in his bag and took out a stone and slung it and struck the Philistine on his forehead. The stone sank into his forehead, and he fell on his face to the ground.

So David prevailed over the Philistine with a sling and with a stone, and struck the Philistine and killed him. There was no sword in the hand of David. Then David ran and stood over the Philistine and took his sword and drew it out of its sheath and killed him and cut off his head with it. When the Philistines saw that their champion was dead, they fled. And the men of Israel and Judah rose with a shout and pursued the Philistines as far as Gath and the gates of Ekron, so that the wounded Philistines fell on the way from Shaaraim as far as Gath and Ekron. And the people of Israel came back from chasing the Philistines, and they plundered their camp. And David took the head of the Philistine and brought it to Jerusalem, but he put his armor in his tent.

As soon as Saul saw David go out against the Philistine, he said to Abner, the commander of the army, "Abner, whose son is this youth?" And Abner said, "As your soul lives, O king, I do not know." And the king said, "Inquire whose son the boy is." And as soon as David returned from the striking down of the Philistine, Abner took him, and brought him before Saul with the head of the Philistine in his hand. And Saul said to him, "Whose son are you, young man?" And David answered, "I am the son of your servant Jesse the Bethlehemite."

PART ONE

THE PROBLEM

1

THE WRONG PLACE AT THE WRONG TIME

"Now the Philistines gathered their armies . . . at Socoh, which belongs to Judah" (1 Samuel 17:1).

What were the Philistines doing in Socoh? They had no business being just nine miles from Jerusalem. This was Israel's land. God gave it to them.

So why were the Philistines where they didn't belong? Very simply: because Israel was weak. It was their own fault. God had given them everything they needed to live securely within their borders yet they continually ignored God and His resources.

God promised blessings on the people if they faithfully followed God's ways—many children, abundant harvests, multiplying flocks. Further, "The Lord will cause your enemies who rise against you to be defeated before you" (Deuteronomy 28:7). In contrast, if they didn't obey God's commands, the consequences were harsh, including this: "The Lord will cause you to be defeated before your enemies" (Deuteronomy 28:25). So it's clear why Israel faced the problem of an invading and occupying foreign army.

Furthermore, this wasn't a fair fight. This was a holocaust waiting to happen. The Philistine army had all the modern weapons—swords and spears and chariots and armor. The Israelite army had . . . two swords. That's it! Saul and Jonathan were properly armed. The rest of the troops grabbed whatever sticks, hay forks, and other farm implements they could. This was a superpower smugly challenging a defenseless third-world country.

I understand the situation. When I was a boy, Germany invaded my country, the Netherlands. Just like the Philistines, they entered with overwhelming force. The Dutch fought bravely . . . on their bicycles! The Germans countered with air bombardments and paratroopers and tanks. It was no contest. For this Dutch teenager it was humiliating to see German soldiers on every corner. I fought back in my very limited way. But it was dangerous. Resisters who got caught were either shot or shipped to concentration camps.

Well, by now we Christians have surely learned our lessons. Now we are prepared. We would never let our enemies occupy our places of worship or our homes. That may be what we think but the church doesn't seem to be aware of all the devil may throw at us. We are confused and anemic. **The world has invaded our churches and most of us don't even know it.** We have been invaded with a tsunami of information and entertainment pouring into our minds from television and movies and games and Internet and social media. Do we even recognize how feeble we really are?

When I think of the situation today, I recall simpler times when television first came to the Netherlands. It was in the mid 1950s when my Uncle Hoppy (you can read about Uncle Hoppy in my book *God's Smuggler*) ordered one of those black-and-white consoles. The delivery van arrived at his house and two men carried the box into his living room. In large letters on the cardboard packaging was printed this invitation: "Bring the world into your home!" Hoppy read that and yelled, "No! Take it back!" Uncle Hoppy refused to allow the world to invade his home.

Later I thought of Joel 2:9, which tells about a powerful enemy in the day of the Lord: "they climb up into the houses, they enter through the windows like a thief." Well, Uncle Hoppy wasn't going to let the enemy come in!

This sounds a little harsh, doesn't it? Most of us would protest: "You can't isolate yourself." Today's connected world requires everyone to have a computer, Internet, the latest smart phone, and a Kindle or an iPad (or both!). If you agree with that statement, you may have a serious problem.

I know many parents are concerned that their children will be exposed to filth on the Internet, so they devise schemes and blocks to prevent children from seeing certain programs or websites. In other words, we let the enemy in and then try to confine him. Isn't it better to admit that the enemy is in our living room where he doesn't belong?

Now, don't quit on me here. I'm not naïve and suggesting we completely cut ourselves off from the world. (Indeed I have a television in my office—but no computer or smart phone!) The situation isn't hopeless. We can form a resistance movement. As a teenager, I sabotaged several German vehicles. Big deal! I know that my pranks made very little difference. They were a futile effort, unless . . . unless others also resisted, thousands of others.

It may seem that there is no way to stop the invasion. I love the quote by Martin Luther: "I can't stop the birds from flying around me. But I can prevent them from building a nest in my hair." That's why we need the example of David. He will show us how to start a real resistance movement, even against hopeless odds. But remember, the situation today is *not* hopeless—if we understand what David knew.

FOR REFLECTION: *How have the information and entertainment industries infiltrated our churches and our homes? What effect has this had on your church? Your family?*

2

IMPOSSIBLE ODDS

"Saul and the men of Israel were gathered . . . and drew up in line of battle against the Philistines" (1 Samuel 17:2).

What a sorry, ragtag bunch this Israelite "army" was. The writer of Samuel doesn't belabor the details because earlier (in I Samuel 13:5) he spelled out how unevenly matched the two sides were. The Philistine army consisted of:

- 30,000 chariots
- 6,000 horsemen
- A massive army (more than they could count) fully protected and armed
- Giants—at least five of them (more on them later)

Have you ever watched a cat torture a mouse? It's not much fun. When our cat catches a mouse, he doesn't kill it right away. He plays with it. He lets the mouse run two or three steps and then traps it. He takes his paw and flicks the mouse up in the air. He toys with the mouse, tortures it, until he gets bored. Then with one swift bite he finishes it off. But he probably doesn't eat it.

Some people seem to get great pleasure using their power at the expense of those much weaker. In this case the Philistines were the cat, Israel the pitiful mouse. It makes you wonder why Israel bothered to show up. Surely no one in Saul's company expected victory. All anyone could reasonably hope for was to save his own skin. At least this time they didn't run away. In an earlier confrontation at Micmash, the Israelites lost their nerve entirely and hid in caves, holes, rocks, tombs, and cisterns. Some escaped the country altogether. Today we call it emigration.

The problem was that Israel hadn't properly analyzed the problem. They thought they had an answer to their weakness. "Appoint for us a king," they demanded, so we can be "like all the nations" (1 Samuel 8:5). Their solution: a politician, a handsome military leader, a man.

Israel didn't need a politician. They didn't need a tall, beautiful, well-dressed symbol. They needed a fresh commitment to God. They needed someone who would show them what true faith in God looked like.

Still, God answered their prayers. (When I think about it, maybe we don't really want God to answer all of our prayers.) God gave them a king. After a promising start, things actually got worse.

The prophet Samuel had clearly warned the people that a king would not solve their problems. Kings would draft young men into the army, conscript them as slave labor, lay claim to their best fields and vineyards, and tax their harvests and flocks. Nevertheless, the people were adamant—"Give us a king!"

The answer to their prayer was a tall, handsome, athletic man. Saul looked the part but he failed the heart test. His problem was pride. He didn't know how to take orders, God's orders. In a panic when his army was disintegrating, he performed a sacrifice, which could only be done by a priest. Later Saul received clear instructions to wipe out the Amalakite nation. But Saul compromised, saving their king and choice animals, and then made excuses for his disobedience. Consequently, God abandoned Saul.

Here's the point: **A teenager filled with the Holy Spirit is more powerful than a king that God has abandoned.** Israel chose to trust in politics and found themselves hopelessly adrift. When they were lined up against a superpower, they had no hope of victory.

Is the situation any better today? Aren't too many of us putting our hope in political solutions for everything from job creation to global warming? We look to new laws and court decisions and charismatic leaders who repeat simplistic promises. We put our faith in get-out-the-vote campaigns, community activism, and petition drives. Then we are disappointed when we don't get the expected results.

Media organize the masses with their thirty-second sound bite solutions but they haven't properly analyzed the problem. Aim at nothing and you will hit it every time! Christians are no better. We fight over theology and strategy and policy and, divided, make no difference in our society. That's because Christians don't recognize the real enemy either.

I don't want to discourage you. There *is* an answer. However, we may not recognize it if we don't understand that our pitiful, barely armed forces have no chance against the forces of this world and the devil's demonic legions. Those who do understand the problem can make a difference. *You* can be God's instrument to change the odds. If, that is, you understand God's ways.

FOR REFLECTION: *How do you know that you are putting your trust in God rather than political leaders or systems?*

3

A MOST INTIMIDATING OPPONENT

> *"There came out from the camp of the Philistines a champion named Goliath of Gath"* (1 Samuel 17:4).

Look at him! In verse after verse the Philistine champion is profiled. This warrior:

- is nearly ten feet tall
- wears 125 pounds of armor
- wields a spear that looks like a fence rail, with a spear tip weighing 15 pounds
- carries a bronze sword

He is unbeatable!

That's the point. The enemy always wants you to believe that resistance is futile. You might as well give up right now. Why fight when you know you can't win?

That's the way it is with giants. They want you to believe your eyes and ears. They want you to recognize the impossible odds. But if all you do is rely on your physical senses, you miss the full picture.

The Apostle Paul understood the real enemy and in 2 Corinthians taught that we are not fighting against the giants we see but the single giant we don't see. Our true enemy is the deceiver, the one who inspires every argument and lofty opinion raised up against the knowledge of God (2 Corinthians 10:3–5). Meanwhile we get caught up in our theological battles. Calvinists say we need right doctrine. Pentecostals say we need the baptism of the Spirit. Liturgical denominations emphasize their traditions. We tend to focus on our distinctives and forget that we are one army designed to fight a spiritual enemy that holds the world captive. The giants we see are really just poor images of the real enemy.

No doubt you will protest that Goliath was a real flesh and blood threat to Israel. Today a Christian suffering in persecution feels real pain, prejudice, and rejection. Real flames burn their churches and homes. Inflexible iron bars enclose them in very real prisons. For some today the end is a martyr's death that leaves behind the agony of a grieving spouse, parent, or pastor. These are realities we can't ignore.

Think with me for a minute. If the real enemy is unseen, then just what exactly is going on in the Valley of Elah? As long as we view any Bible story as an isolated incident, we will never gain insight into the real battle. Everything in Scripture is recorded to teach us the character of God, the nature of spiritual warfare, and the way of salvation.

The ultimate spiritual battle began early in Genesis when the serpent (our enemy, the devil) tempted Adam and Eve and they ate the forbidden fruit. The devil told the first couple that now they would know good and evil. That seemed so attractive. He didn't explain they would not have the power to do good nor would they have the power not to do evil.

God declared judgment on the devil: "I will put enmity between you and the woman, and between your offspring and her offspring; he shall bruise your head, and you shall bruise his heel" (Genesis 3:15). **Here is the key to understanding all that follows in the Old**

Testament. The devil's objective is to prevent the promised offspring from being born. If he can do that, he wins and can continue to rule over planet earth. Thus he will do everything in his power to prevent the birth of the Redeemer.

Think back to before Israel gained possession of the Promised Land. Twelve Hebrew spies reported seeing Nephilim and feeling "like grasshoppers" near them (Numbers 13:32–33). The Nephilim refer to ancient giants that were offspring of angelic beings and human women (Genesis 6:4). I don't know how or if they survived the flood—the Scriptures are vague about this. The Bible says "the Nephilim were on the earth in those days, and also afterward" (Genesis 6:4).

Apparently giants resembling the ancient Nephilim were in Canaan. We see brief mentions of them in Joshua. The descendents of Joseph complained that their portion of land was too small. Joshua challenged them to go into the hill country drive out "the Rephaim," a label also given to the Philistine giants (Joshua 17:15). Caleb also confronted giants in the hill country when he drove out the Anakim and claimed his inheritance (Joshua 14:12). So for whatever reason there were giants in the land, and one was taunting Israel.

Now listen to David shouting after he heard Goliath's taunts: "Who is this uncircumcised Philistine?" The question implies the answer. Goliath is a heathen! He has no part of the Kingdom of God. He is an instrument of the devil whose purpose is to subvert the human race and make the birth of Messiah impossible. **If Goliath wins this battle, the genealogy of David is broken and Satan thwarts God's plan.**

By the way, Satan has a backup plan. If Goliath should fail (inconceivable!), he has four brothers and maybe a few cousins who are determined to finish the job.[1] So the stakes are high, only no one realizes just how high.

Perhaps you think it's a different story today. Christ has come.

He has redeemed us. He has established His Kingdom. However, the devil's rebellion persists. He continues to try to thwart the advancement of God's Kingdom throughout the world. He works constantly to prevent the return of Jesus to claim what is rightfully His.

Do you recognize the spiritual warfare? The evidence is all around you. Just watch the news—you'll see.

The devil has lost but he is not dead and he continues to take casualties. God calls His people to resist the devil. Will you step forward?

FOR REFLECTION: *What evidence do you see of Satan's rebellion today? How is he trying to thwart the advancement of God's Kingdom?*

4

A WAR OF WORDS

> *"He stood and shouted to the ranks of Israel,' . . .
> I defy the ranks of Israel this day. Give me a man,
> that we may fight together'"* (1 Samuel 17:8, 10).

The giant doesn't bother to use his superior weaponry. Instead, he shouts. He uses words with the purpose of intimidating Israel. It works—Israel listens to the lies, lies mixed with a little truth.

Listen to Goliath's taunt: "Why have you come out to draw up for battle?" (v. 8). This is a lie! Israel did not come out to make war against the Philistines. The Philistines invaded Israel. They occupied places where they did not belong. Goliath proposed the solution to a problem the Philistines caused.

This battle should really be fought in enemy territory. Not in Socoh. Not near Jerusalem. Never in the Promised Land. Four hundred years earlier Israel had every right to invade Gaza and drive out the occupants. If they had done so under God's command and Joshua's leadership, there would have been no Philistine problem.

We Christians must realize that we are fighting the wrong battles in the wrong places. Too many battles are fought in our churches and families. Battles should never be fought there. We should be unified as Christians. We fight battles in our hearts against sin when we should be free from sin. Holy and united we should take the battle to a culture that fiercely resists the rule of God—outside our churches, outside our families.

Well, that's just the start: "Am I not a Philistine, and are you not servants of Saul?" Goliath is telling Israel that they aren't really free. Goliath looks with disdain at Israel's king who at this moment is hiding in his tent. Saul is nothing, so by implication the Israelites are "servants of nothing." The giant has no idea of the significance of this statement. He really is saying that Israel is spiritually inept. They aren't servants of a mighty God. They are slaves of an inept, cowardly king.

Well, Goliath got that right! I doubt he knew about God's judgment in Genesis 3:15, but the devil used him as a mouthpiece. The devil really is saying, "Out of you bunch of little cowards there will never come anyone who will bruise my head. I'm so big you can't even touch me. Choose a man if you want, if you can find someone. It won't matter because I will crush him." The stage is set for the devil's "final solution."

So the significance of this battle has been grossly underestimated. The prophet Isaiah observed, "O Lord our God, other lords besides you have ruled over us" (Isaiah 26:13). This is a vital insight into spiritual warfare. How casually we sing worship songs like "All to Jesus I Surrender." Then we leave the church sanctuary and on Monday go back to slaving for more money and serving the "right" political party and surrendering to the dominant cultural influences around us.

Frankly, here is the whole point of this conflict. **Israel has a choice: to serve Almighty God or serve the agents of their archenemy, the devil.** Tragically, no one except a teenage boy understood the stakes.

FOR REFLECTION: *In the spiritual conflict raging today, what is the evidence that you are an agent of Almighty God rather than a servant of the dominant culture?*

5

TOTAL BRAINWASHING

"For forty days the Philistine came forward and took his stand, morning and evening" (1 Samuel 17:16).

The Philistines are engaged in psychological warfare and it works. Brilliantly! Their spokesman sneers, "Why have you come out to draw up for battle?" (v. 8). The giant's words sting. Israel has no weapons. They are hopelessly outmanned. Israel must have realized: *We are not here to fight a battle. At best, this is a show. At worst, we are about to be slaughtered. Either prospect is hopeless.*

This continues day after day, week after week. Over and over Goliath repeats one message. Eighty times! Let's call this what it really is: brainwashing. Over and over the enemy shouts:

- You are slaves.
- You are powerless.
- Try to fight me; I will crush you.
- You will never be free.
- You will always be weak.
- You will never have any weapons.
- You are worthless.
- You call yourselves people of God—how pathetic!

Day after day the lies are repeated. The Philistines don't have to fight. They don't need to take any risks. They've already won the battle of words. It's a rout: eighty to nothing.

When we look around the world, we are afraid of weapons of mass destruction. We must prevent Iran from gaining nuclear weapons. We must stop al-Qaeda from getting biological weapons. How can we prevent another terrorist attack like 9/11 in the United States or 7/7 in the UK or the Madrid train bombing?

Certainly various countries and terrorist groups pose serious threats. However, we really ought to be scared of something more powerful than any jihadist movement or emerging nuclear power. I'm talking about *word* weapons. Jesus said, "Do not fear those who kill the body but cannot kill the soul" (Matthew 10:28). Atom bombs can kill only the body. Words destroy people's minds. Our world is filled with destructive messages. Ideologies like Communism and Islamic fundamentalism claim millions. Philosophies embedded in many university courses try to capture our young people. Words, words, words! And the people of God say almost nothing. We are so intimidated.

How many Christians believe these lies: You are powerless. You can never cope with your problems. You can't change. You will always be sick. You will never have victory over sin—so give up! You will never live the life God wants you to live.

Eighty times and more we hear these messages. Let's admit it: we are brainwashed.

But there is a solution. We must fight these words with the Word. David knew and used the Word. The problem is that we don't know the Scriptures.

On my first trip to Czechoslovakia, I sat next to a Communist party member on a bus. He had debated many Christians and, when he quickly realized I was a follower of Jesus, he challenged me by asking, "Have you read the whole Bible?"

"Sure!" I answered. "Several times."

The Communist leader was aghast. "I've asked many Christians that question. You are the first one who tells me he has read the whole Bible even once."

If we haven't read our Bibles, then no wonder we are ignorant. Ask Christians individually what their message is for the world today and many admit they have no message. Do you have a message? Every Christian, without exception, should have a message. "Take up the sword of the Spirit," writes the Apostle Paul, "which is the word of God" (Ephesians 6:16–17). Take the Word! **God's Word is infinitely superior to the giant's word!** The enemy doesn't want you to have the Word. But why should he tell you what to have and what to believe?

The issue here is the power of God. In Revelation we read that Jesus will hand over the Kingdom of God to His Father. This is the culmination of the spiritual battle. All power will be God's. He will reign over all creation. This is what the devil is determined to prevent.

The Israelites should never have been intimidated by Philistine rules. Their enemy decreed that no Israelite could own a sword. If a farmer needed a mattock or axe sharpened, he had to travel to a Philistine blacksmith and pay dearly for the service. What an outrage! This was an impossible and ridiculous situation. Israel should have established blacksmith shops and forged weapons to protect themselves against invaders. That was their right!

The enemy thinks he can decide whether or not we have our weapon. When I hear governments declaring that the Bible is a forbidden book, I rebel. This is never the will of God. So when Communist countries decided they would determine how many Bibles, if any, were available for Christians, I refused to accept their declarations. I became "God's Smuggler." I believed, and still believe, that every Christian has a basic human right to have his own Bible in his own language. This is the reason I am a member of Wycliffe Bible Translators. Their aim is to provide every tribe in the world Scripture in their own language.

In many Muslim countries the situation is even worse than it ever was in Communist countries. It's harder to get Bibles into Saudi Arabia today than into Russia in the 1960s. What are we going to do about this? We must not allow any religion or government to limit or regulate access to God's Word.

So here are a couple of questions. Are you armed and ready for battle? Are you listening to the enemy's brainwashing or are you feeding on the Word of God? The answer to these questions will ultimately determine the outcome of today's conflicts.

FOR REFLECTION: *What evidence do you see today that words are brainwashing people's minds? Using the Scriptures, how can you resist these messages?*

6

WHERE'S THE MAN?

"I defy the ranks of Israel this day. Give me a man, that we may fight together" (1 Samuel 17:10).

There is absolutely no doubt who had to go fight Goliath. Everyone knew it was Saul. He was the people's champion. It made perfect sense. But where was the champion of Israel? He was hiding!

Here are Saul's qualifications:

- He was a head taller than anyone else in Israel.
- The Lord chose him to be Israel's king.
- Apparently he began his reign as a humble man.
- Samuel had thoroughly instructed him on the Lord's expectations of a king.
- He was surrounded by men of valor whose hearts were touched by God.
- His son Jonathan was loyal and a valiant warrior.
- He was equipped with the necessary armor and weapons.

Look at the list (you can read it for yourself in 1 Samuel 10:23–26) and you have to wonder how Saul could possibly fail. This was the battle Saul was born to fight. He had every advantage but he failed miserably because he lacked character. Saul was a man of the people, not a man of God.

Character is what a person is when he or she is alone, in the dark, lying in bed. What does a person think about when sleep won't come? Does he pray? Does she scheme? Where does his heart take him? You may not be able to read a person's mind, but his or her behavior will reveal the true character. **Character is forged in secret and revealed in crisis.**

The personal character of Saul and of David showed up on the battlefield for all to see. Saul failed the character test by failing to obey God. Meanwhile, David's character was built up as he fulfilled his responsibility of caring for his father's sheep. What David did with the sheep in secret no one knew. Oh, but God knew!

Saul's problem was that he didn't follow God's clear instructions. Just one example will suffice. Saul was instructed to go and destroy the Amalekites—every one of them, man, woman, child, infant, ox, sheep, camel, and donkey. This is pretty clear. So Saul went and sort of obeyed. He killed *most* of the Amalekites. He just spared the king and the best animals.

God pronounced judgment on Saul through the prophet Samuel. Saul could have repented but he made excuses instead: "The people took of the spoil, sheep and oxen . . . to sacrifice to the LORD your God" (1 Samuel 15:21). Actually, that wasn't an excuse. It was a lie. Saul's heart is revealed with the statement, the Lord *your* God. The Lord is Samuel's God, but not Saul's God.

God's judgment is swift. "Because you have rejected the word of the LORD, he has also rejected you from being king" (1 Samuel 15:23).

On the battlefield Saul was cowering in his tent because he was no longer God's man and he knew it. "Now the Spirit of the LORD departed from Saul, and a harmful spirit from the LORD tormented him" (1 Samuel 16:14). So Saul was in no position to fight the giant. He knew in his heart it was futile.

Saul's weakness of character reflected the nation's weakness as well. Israel as a whole lacked godly character. What Israel desperately needed was a man of God, not a man out of sorts with God.

The world is constantly looking for a man or a woman who will step up and provide real leadership. We long for someone who will take charge and solve the world's problems. In country after country, we see politicians make bold promises, offer solutions, and inevitably disappoint the masses. We have all sorts of contests—we call them reality shows—looking for survivors, looking for heroes, looking for a real man and a real woman. Of course, none of the winners, none of the athletic heroes, none of the movie stars provide the salvation the world longs for.

Give me a man! God answered that prayer. He gave the world that Man, and they crucified Him. God continues to answer that prayer by giving to the world people in whom Jesus lives. Any Christian, man or woman, can be God's answer to the world's need, because the answer is Jesus, who lives in those who have received Him. If you let Him, He will forge your character. Then you can be Jesus to a desperate world. You may be the only Jesus they will ever see.

The issue isn't results. The issue is: Am I willing to be the one God uses? The choice is yours. If you refuse to choose, then you have chosen to deny Christ.

If you choose to be God's man or woman, you will likely find yourself walking the path He walked. The world hated Jesus. So we shouldn't be surprised when the world hates His followers.

Will you accept the challenge to follow Jesus wherever He takes you?

FOR REFLECTION: *How are you showing Jesus to the world around you (your family, your neighbors, in your work place)?*

7

WHO'S AFRAID OF THE BIG BAD GIANT?

*"When Saul and all Israel heard these words . . .
they were dismayed and greatly afraid"
(1 Samuel 17:11).*

Saul was right to be dismayed and afraid. God's Spirit had departed from him.

Israel had every reason to be dismayed and afraid because they were focused on the wrong things. They were listening to the wrong words. Brainwashing, when we continuously expose ourselves to it, immobilizes us and leads to hopelessness.

Fear has sometimes been defined as "False Evidence Appearing Real." Well, the evidence before Israel feels very real. He's nine-and-a-half feet tall. You can't get much more real than that. But this is only a physical reality. Israel doesn't see what's happening on a spiritual level. You need spiritual eyes to recognize the real battle.

I don't consider myself a pacifist but I can observe how easy it is to start a war without realizing what the results may be. So we choose sides without understanding the real issues. Some readers won't like this example, but when the United States invaded Iraq and toppled Saddam Hussein, did anyone consider the cost to the church in Iraq? The fact is that the church was devastated and

Christians were scattered. More than 60 percent of all believers in Iraq have been displaced.

Jump ahead a few years to the events known as Arab Spring. People in Tunisia, Yemen, Egypt, and Syria were rising up in revolt against autocratic rulers. We applauded their courage, but what was happening underneath the revolutions? What were the devil's intentions? How was God using this for the advancement of His Kingdom? **What did these events mean for the church in those countries?** These are the questions we should ask. These are the issues that should dominate our prayers.

As I write this, Russia and China may be forming a new military alliance. There have been riots in at least twenty Middle Eastern countries over the stupid film *Innocence of Muslims*. In America a bitter presidential race is being fought. Supporters on both sides worry about the consequences if the other guy wins. Meanwhile the European Union teeters, wondering about the impact if Greece defects or if Spain or Italy or Ireland default on their loans. By the time you read this, the big news stories may have changed, but there will no doubt be plenty of reason to be afraid. When we focus on the surface problems, our daily news gives us plenty of reasons to be scared.

Any action based on fear is wrong. If we call in F-16s and drop a bomb on Goliath's head, will that end our problem? No, you will have an enemy that despises you. They will seek revenge. You will live in constant fear. So the enemy is actually strengthened by our actions. We see this so often and it helps explain the reason there is so much hatred and so much turmoil in the world. There must be a better way.

Someone needs to step forward and lead us back to God. Only then will the cycle of fear end. The problem for Israel as they confront Goliath is that the man of God has not appeared yet. Israel is stuck in a ruthless cycle of intimidation, brainwashing, and fear. Their king is looking for a miracle—not a God-miracle—rather a stronger nation that will come to his rescue. That's what the world's leaders do today. They look for a strong man like Vladimir Putin of Russia. They seek an alliance with a military power like the United States or China. But to forge such alliances, a leader must offer something in return. Saul has nothing to offer. There are no concessions left to make. Saul is already defeated.

David wasn't about to make any concessions, either. He had already won!

It's time to meet the hero of our story.

FOR REFLECTION: *What are you afraid of? How do you handle your fears?*

PART TWO

INTRODUCING THE MAN OF GOD

8

WHERE DID HE COME FROM?

> *"Now David was the son of... Jesse, who had eight sons"* (1 Samuel 17:12).

It is tempting to think that David was mighty brave to step forward and confront Goliath. I don't believe that explains our hero. There were other brave men who could have fought the giant. Bravery alone doesn't insure victory.

Where does God's person come from? It's hard to draw conclusions from David's background. When David was born, Saul had already been king for several years. David was the son of Jesse, an Ephrathite of Bethlehem. There were seven older brothers. I can't help but wonder if David was a surprise child. Unexpected? Maybe. Unwanted? I don't know. From the family's actions, he appears to be an afterthought.

One thing we do know—David was a boy after God's heart. Samuel told Saul that God was looking for such a person. Was David conscious that he was a person after God's heart? I kind of doubt it. But God recognized it.

How did David's spiritual journey begin? Maybe during a trip to the tabernacle, or was it due to Jesse's influence? Perhaps the love of his mother influenced him—it's interesting that absolutely no mention is made of her. Is it possible that the prophet Samuel's leadership had had an impact on David? But the prophet had no knowledge of David until God sent him to anoint him as Saul's replacement.

The songs David wrote reveal his heart for God but they don't reveal how he began his spiritual journey. Did it start with a dream? Or the witness of a neighbor? Perhaps the seed was planted when Jesse's family celebrated Passover. Then David would have heard the story of Moses rescuing the Israelites from slavery and leading them across the Red Sea. If that was the case—reading from the Torah, hearing a story from his father—it took root and blossomed into faith.

Maybe David's heart was kindled with love for God when he gazed at the stars one clear night as the sheep slept in the wilderness. "The heavens declare the glory of God," he wrote in Psalm 19. "And the sky above proclaims his handiwork" (v. 1). So perhaps God's creation spoke to David and opened his spirit. Whatever the source, David acted on the light he saw. That was more than could be said for the priests and Levites who should have known the Law of Moses, or for the royal court that had heard Samuel's instructions when King Saul was inaugurated.

One thing we do see of David is that he was a man of principle. Perhaps he had learned integrity from his father. David's character was evident in the way he cared for his father's sheep. He would protect them no matter what the cost. That was his responsibility and he would not let his father down. His thinking was: *The sheep belong to my father, so I can't lose one!* David brought this same sense of responsibility to the battlefield.

What does it mean to be a man or woman after God's heart? For one thing, you will make proper moral and ethical decisions, especially in these confusing times. David did not emerge as God's man because he killed Goliath. David's actions to defeat Goliath were the natural result of his principles. It was his character that made him fearless. He was committed to doing the right thing regardless of personal cost.

But moral rectitude wasn't enough. Many people live upright lives yet do nothing for God. To explain David we must delve deeper than that. David wanted to *know* God and not just know about God. As we read the Psalms (half of them are written by David) we discover what was in his thinking, his commentary on the world, how he gained perspective by praising the Almighty, and also how he released his emotions. We could write a whole book on this subject. Let's just look at a five examples:

"You, O Lord, are a shield about me, my glory, and the lifter of my head" (Psalm 3:3).

"You have given me relief when I was in distress. Be gracious to me and hear my prayer!" (Psalm 4:1).

"I will give thanks to the Lord with my whole heart; I will recount all of your wonderful deeds" (Psalm 9:1).

"Why, O Lord, do you stand far away? Why do you hide yourself in times of trouble?" (Psalm10:1).

"The fool says in his heart, 'There is no God'. . . . The Lord looks down from heaven on the children of man, to see if there are any who understand, who seek after God" (Psalm 14:1–2).

God looked for a man who would act solely as His representative with no other motive. Until he reached the battlefield and saw Goliath, David may not have realized that God needed a victory. But God let him know that he should act on His behalf. This must be the reason for any initiative in spiritual battle. To carry out God's will, our motivation must have heaven's endorsement.

FOR REFLECTION: *Why would you say you are a man or woman after God's heart? If you can't say you are a person after God's heart, how can you change that?*

9

A VITAL COMPONENT

"As for me, far be it from me that I should sin against the LORD by ceasing to pray for you" (1 Samuel 12:23).

Before there was David, there was a prayer warrior. Understand, Samuel was old. He was retired. He believed his work was finished. He had served his people well for decades. He began his service in the tabernacle as a little boy. Over the years he'd been priest, prophet, judge, military leader, and counselor. He'd traveled throughout the region fulfilling his responsibilities. He'd led a revival. Then he'd anointed his successor, Saul, the first king of Israel. Samuel was a beloved leader, a man full of integrity, a man of character. By now he was old and tired and had earned the right to live out his final days in peace. However, these were not peaceful days.

When Samuel delivered his farewell speech, he reminded the people of all the great things God had done for the nation. God has been their king for hundreds of years. Yet the people had demanded a "real" king. They got their ideal leader—rich, tall, strong, handsome. Saul was everything anyone could want in a chief executive.

A VITAL COMPONENT

But though God had given Israel a king, God was still in charge. Ultimately the king answered to Him. The Lord had appointed Saul. The Lord could also remove him.

Samuel exhorted the people: Be faithful to the Lord and all will go well. Worship worthless idols and you will feel His wrath. In this context Samuel made a promise: "Far be it from me that I should sin against the LORD by ceasing to pray for you." So even though Samuel retired, one activity never stopped. He prayed—constantly. When a person has communed with God over decades, he or she cannot give that up.

No doubt Samuel thought back over his life and reflected on all God had done. Probably the first voice he remembered was that of his mother, Hannah. He could remember as a toddler cuddling up against her on her lap as she told him the story of his miraculous birth. Samuel was the answer to her prayers. Before he was even born, she had dedicated him to God for His service. So when as a young boy, he was delivered to the tabernacle, he felt homesick for a while but also knew that this was where he belonged.

Eli, the grossly overweight old priest, was like a father to him. Samuel remembered his voice too, particularly the day he chastised his two grown sons. Samuel knew he shouldn't have eavesdropped, but Eli's voice carried and he was angry. "Why do you do such things?" Eli had said. "It is no good report that I hear . . . If someone sins against a man, God will mediate for him; but if someone sins against the LORD, who can intercede for him?" (1 Samuel 2:23–25). Samuel didn't yet understand all that Eli's sons were doing wrong but he realized they were definitely not a good example to follow.

Then how could he forget the night he first heard the Voice. He was lying near the Ark of the Covenant, unable to sleep. The Voice was soft, calling his name. *Eli needs me,* Samuel thought. But it wasn't Eli. God was calling Samuel. He quickly learned to recognize that Voice and many nights he lay awake, hoping for another revelation from God. He wasn't disappointed!

How Samuel loved that Voice. He prayed every day, longing always to hear from God. Sure, Samuel petitioned God, but his prayer was much more of an ongoing conversation. He may have been finished with his work but he never ended the conversation. So he could tell God how sad he felt about Saul. The humble man whom he had anointed king had grown so full of himself that he'd built a monument—not to God but to himself. God whispered back to Samuel—He too was sorry He had made Saul king of Israel.

There was nothing else Samuel could do except pray. Not to pray would be a sin against God. So Samuel prayed against the will and plans of King Saul.

Are you disturbed by events in the world today? Do you think the political leaders in your country are on the wrong path? Don't complain, pray! That's our responsibility. That's our privilege. **We can accomplish more on our knees than can the leaders of any superpower. Do we believe this?**

> Satan trembles when he sees
> the weakest saint upon his knees.
> The gates of hell shall tremble when
> the devil sees many praying men.
> —Source Unknown

FOR REFLECTION: *How would you describe your prayer life? Do you pray expecting God to respond?*

10

HOW TO PRAY FOR A FAILING LEADER

> *"The L*ORD *has sought out a man after his own heart"* (1 Samuel 13:14).

Just what was Samuel praying for? We don't know for sure but we can make an intelligent guess. Samuel was praying for a real leader! We can see the disappointment Samuel felt with King Saul. "You have acted foolishly," he chided after the king made the unauthorized sacrifice.

Clearly Samuel understood what was required. "Keep the commandments the Lord gave you." Simple. Unambiguous. Everything was spelled out in the Torah, the first five books of our Bible. There was a clear division of responsibility, and rules for justice and worship and health. When he had opportunity, he also instructed the people. For years he taught them the good and right ways. He exhorted the people to "fear the LORD and serve him faithfully with all your heart" (1 Samuel 12:24). Apparently the Israelites didn't pay much attention, so Samuel prayed some more.

Saul knew what he had to do, and if he had a question, all he had to do was ask. Samuel would gladly coach him. Saul was accountable to one boss—God. He failed because he became his own authority.

When he faced a crisis, he didn't call out for God's help, he figured things out himself. What a mess he made!

From appearances only it seemed that King Saul was doing okay. He looked regal when he appeared in public for worship of Almighty God. He led the army to many victories. He was a valiant fighter and his army held back Moab, the Ammonites, Edom, and for a time, even the Philistines. If you watched the news and read the papers, it would have appeared that Saul, while not perfect, was a good enough leader.

Samuel knew better. God had given him a glimpse into Saul's heart. It was corrupt. Saul wasn't fit to rule God's people, so we can imagine what Samuel prayed. *Lord, Saul is corrupt. He has not obeyed Your commands. We need a man after Your own heart to rule this nation. Lord, would You make Saul that man? Would You soften his heart so that he listens to You? Will You make him the kind of man You want him to be?*

Lord, if Saul will not change, then will You replace him? Will You bring the right person to the throne? Lord, just who is the right person? Wherever he is, prepare him now for the throne. May he be brave, a warrior. May he love You and communicate with You just like we communicate. May he be a good leader, a man of character. Yes, a man after Your own heart.

Now Samuel was a prophet so he did have an advantage of often knowing what was on God's mind. But God didn't reveal everything to him. **Samuel knew the problem but he didn't know the solution. Certainly that was the focus of his prayer.** He saw two options: a transformed Saul or a new leader with the right heart. Actually, there was a third option, but the people had already rejected that. They could fire Saul and make God their king again but that wasn't going to happen.

So Samuel prayed and waited. Whatever the crisis you see in the world, you can do what Samuel did—pray and wait on God.

Because Samuel prayed, he heard the Voice once more.

FOR REFLECTION: *When you look at the world, how do you pray? How are you praying for the leaders of your nation, your community, your church?*

11

PREPARE TO BE GOD'S ANSWER

> *"The LORD said to Samuel, 'How long will you grieve over Saul, since I have rejected him from being king over Israel? Fill your horn with oil, and go. I will send you to Jesse the Bethlehemite, for I have provided for myself a king among his sons'"* (1 Samuel 16:1).

Are you prepared for God's answer to your prayers? Here's an even tougher question: Are you prepared to *be* God's answer to your prayers?

Despite his age, Samuel had to come out of retirement. God gave the prophet one more assignment: Stop grieving. Get up. Go! I have work for you to do.

There comes a time when prayer moves into action. Sometimes that takes years. Samuel didn't give up praying for Saul or praying for the nation. But he also listened. **Samuel didn't just pray for his nation; he was ready to be God's instrument to rescue the nation.**

You may be thinking "I can't slay giants in this world. I'm not a David. I'm old. I'm not qualified. I'm weak. I've done all I can. I'm

_____." Fill in the blank. But there is something you *can* do. You can pray! Young or old, rich or poor, weak or strong, all of us have a responsibility to pray.

There are plenty of problems facing the world today. We can worry about them. We can talk about them. We can form organizations that pressure politicians to solve them. We can give money. We can write blogs. The one thing we *must* do is pray.

If Samuel doesn't pray, David is never identified as the solution to Israel's problem. Do you see the connection?

Are you frustrated with your nation's chief executive? Pray.

Are you fearful concerning your city's poverty or crime sprees? Pray.

Are you worried about your nation's moral fiber? Pray.

Are you fretting about your children and their walk with God? Pray.

Pray and listen. The two go together. Then be ready to act—not to rush out and solve the problem yourself. Saul did that when facing the Philistines in another battle (see 1 Samuel 13). The Philistines were about to attack, and Israel's army had scattered to the hills. Only a few hundred soldiers remained, and Saul had no idea how long they would stay with him. Before the battle was to begin, Samuel was to offer a sacrifice, but when he didn't show up at the appointed time, Saul felt he had to act and so he did a stupid thing. He offered the sacrifice. God's instructions were clear—the priest, in this case Samuel, must perform the sacrifice. Saul needed to wait.

Saul disobeyed because it was the "logical" thing to do. This was Samuel's "uh-oh" moment. When he finally showed up, all he could do was proclaim God's verdict. Saul was foolish. Stupid! "Saul, if only you had obeyed, God would have established your kingdom over Israel for all time. Now your kingdom will not endure" (1 Samuel 13:13–14).

So pray. Wait patiently. But be prepared to act when God speaks.

Samuel thought his work was finished. He was retired. Still he prayed. God answered his prayers by giving him one final assignment.

"You've mourned long enough. Get up and go to Jesse of Bethlehem. I have chosen one of his sons to be king."

Samuel wasn't sure he had heard right. "I can't do that! If Saul hears about it he will kill me," he protested.

God said in essence: "Don't argue with Me. Just go and do it." So Samuel did as the Lord instructed him.

FOR REFLECTION: *How will you know if and when God wants you to be a part of His answer to your prayers?*

12

THE ANTIDOTE TO FEAR

"Samuel did what the LORD commanded and came to Bethlehem. The elders of the city came to meet him trembling" (1 Samuel 16:4).

While Samuel was praying, what was life like in Bethlehem? You have to wonder by the way the town "welcomed" him. The city came out trembling, asking, "Do you come peaceably?" Doesn't that seem like a strange question? Samuel was a revered spiritual leader. For at least fifty years he had built a reputation of integrity. Why wouldn't Bethlehem welcome him warmly?

Of course, Samuel wasn't surprised by the cool reception. He even questioned God about the assignment. "If Saul hears of this, he will kill me," he said (see 1 Samuel 16:2).

Why was everyone so afraid? Because the nation of Israel was sick. They had rejected their rightful king (God) for a fraud. The consequences were predictable—Samuel had warned them. "These will be the ways of the king who will reign over you," he'd said. "He will take your sons and appoint them to his chariots and to be his horsemen and to run before his chariots. And he will appoint for himself commanders of thousands . . . and some to plow his ground and to reap his harvest. . . . He will take your daughters to be perfumers and cooks and bakers. He will take the best of your fields and vineyards and olive orchards and give them to his servants. He will take the tenth of your grain and of your vineyards. . . . He will take . . . the best of your young men and your donkeys, and put them to his work" (1 Samuel 8:11–16). On and on it goes.

Some of these prophesies had come to pass under Saul. He had become a dictator. Sooner or later that's what happens when a ruler detaches himself from God's authority. Without a legal framework to restrict his powers, he can do whatever he wants. Life under Saul couldn't have been pleasant.

Samuel's assignment was to anoint Saul's successor and that was a problem. Samuel was scared. Bethlehem was scared. So God provided a cover. Samuel was to disguise his purpose by bringing a heifer with him and telling the city's elders that he had come to sacrifice to the Lord. Sometimes even God goes underground!

Question: Do we get the leader we deserve? Sometimes we do. Israel got the leader they asked for, and as Samuel had predicted, they were now crying out to God because of it. However, here's an interesting twist. Samuel had said, "The Lord will not answer you in that day" (1 Samuel 8:18). However, Samuel prayed, and God applied grace to give Israel a leader they did *not* deserve.

We're about to meet our young hero. At this point he's in the fields, tending sheep, unaware of Samuel's visit and oblivious to the fact that later in the day his life would dramatically change. He was protected somewhat from the attitude of the day. If you are out alone, away from the town gossip, avoiding the dinner table conversation criticizing the king, with no access to BBC or CNN, you can focus your mind on more productive things.

It's important to counter the negative thinking of our age and not join in the spiral of complaint, talking problems to death, which is not very productive. If we don't, we can expect fear and despair to result. Paralysis is likely. Or some human reaction which will lead us in the wrong direction.

Samuel prayed. David learned and grew. Both were ready to respond when God's door opened.

I'm not suggesting we ignore the problems of the world around us. **I am proposing something more constructive than endless complaints. That's prayer.** We pray intelligently by feeding our minds with thoughts from God, which come from Scripture.

How much are you feeding at this rich trough of God's feast? Our Father's Book will help us pray and prepare us for action.

FOR REFLECTION: *What problems do you like to complain about? How can you turn those complaints into prayers?*

13

FIRST IMPRESSIONS CAN BE WRONG

*"Then Samuel said to Jesse,
'Are all your sons here?'" (1 Samuel 16:11).*

Of the hundreds of thousands of men living in Israel, why did God choose an immature teenager as his man? Samuel figured, logically, that they needed a godly man, a mature man who could lead! So the candidates lined up in front of Samuel—the seven sons of Jesse.

I've often wondered why Jesse didn't include David in the lineup of his sons. Did he figure David had no chance of being chosen? Was he embarrassed by the lad? Was there a stigma attached to his tending sheep? Perhaps Jesse was protecting David from his brothers' constant verbal abuse. Maybe David was adopted. I've even wondered if maybe David was illegitimate. While there is no evidence of that in Scripture, it's a possibility. In any case, David was a "P.S." to Jesse's seven "perfect" sons.

The "experts" may not have thought much of David, but God had a different perspective. God saw what Jesse, his seven sons, and the city of Bethlehem couldn't see. Initially even Samuel missed it, and his experience should have made him more aware.

FIRST IMPRESSIONS CAN BE WRONG

What did Samuel see? The sons of Jesse lined up before him, probably the oldest at the front and the others stair-stepped down to the youngest. Immediately Samuel was drawn to Eliab. Here he is: tall, strong, handsome, full-grown, mature. This is the man!

No! After all the troubles with Saul and all of Samuel's prayers, he should have known better than to look only at the outward appearance. We've seen what happens when a leader is chosen by size and looks. God explains: "Do not consider his appearance or his height, for I have rejected him. The LORD does not look at the things man looks at. Man looks at the outward appearance, but the LORD looks at the heart" (1 Samuel 16:7 NIV).

So Samuel examined the next son, Abinadab. No, not him.

Okay, what about Shammah? Nope! The Lord hadn't chosen this one.

The Scriptures don't even bother to name the next four sons. They are all rejected. Why didn't God just cut to the chase? Why the charade of looking over all seven sons? God could have just revealed to Samuel that none of them were qualified. He could have saved time by revealing that Jesse was holding back one son.

No, God wanted the drama. Who was His choice? Drum roll, please. This is the ultimate reality show. *Survivor* meets *The Bachelor*. The first seven sons of Jesse got voted off the island before we even meet the "lucky" winner.

Frankly these reality shows do the same thing Samuel and Israel did. Some things really haven't changed in three thousand years. We judge the outside. We can't see into hearts, and this is the reason God must make the choice.

When I was studying at the WEC Missionary Training College, there was a student, Lesley, who by appearances didn't have much future in missions. In fact some of us wondered why he was even admitted to missionary school.

Billy Graham came to Glasgow for a campaign, and we were all recruited to be counselors. On a night we were scheduled to work, we arrived early and entered the arena, which quickly filled to capacity. People continued to arrive and had to stand outside. Among them was Lesley who had arrived after us and couldn't get into the arena.

Seeing the problem Dr. Graham went outside, stood on a balcony, and preached to the crowd. As was his practice, he gave an invitation. However, there was a slight problem. All the counselors were inside the arena. Except Lesley! Boy did he take advantage of the opportunity, counseling more than two hundred people, helping many of them surrender to Jesus. God got the last laugh that night. The least promising student, from our perspective, saw more fruit than the rest of us combined.

C. T. Studd, founder of World Evangelization Crusade (WEC), used to say: "Despise not men or things, however weak or small. God loves to choose and mightily use what men count nothing at all." So God picked David.

We might call it predestination or election. That's true. However, the lesson isn't predestination but rather a question for each of us: Is God calling me? **Yes, God is calling you!** And note that youth does not disqualify anyone from ministry. David is the youngest. He's an afterthought to everyone except God. God chose the most "insignificant" person and prepared him in solitude as he cared for Jesse's sheep.

We could look at the seven older brothers and say they were rejected. That's not the point. God called David to be king. All seven brothers were called to serve in some way. All could have another job if they let God use them.

It's shortsighted to complain when you aren't chosen. You might be chosen later. Consider the parable of the workers in the field. Some were not hired until the eleventh hour, but all were paid the same wage. They kept waiting. No one had hired them (chosen them), but they persevered. So the fact that God chose David was not a final judgment for the seven older brothers. God was not saying He could never use them. He was saying that for the job of king, David was the right choice.

> FOR REFLECTION: *Are you ready for God to choose you? Are you preparing for that day when God will call you to face your Goliath?*

14

WHAT WAS JESSE THINKING?

> *"David said to Saul, 'Your servant used to keep sheep for his father. And when there came a lion, or a bear, and took a lamb from the flock, I went after him and struck him and delivered it out of his mouth. And if he arose against me, I caught him by his beard and struck him and killed him'"*
> *(1 Samuel 17:34–35).*

Why was David a man after God's heart? What exactly was happening with David all alone in the fields with his sheep? Let's take a look.

David had barely reached puberty. He'd endured a hot and busy day herding his father's flock of sheep. Now the thirsty sheep drank contentedly from a pool of still water that had formed at the bank of a cold mountain stream. Leaning back against a rock, he fiddled with his sling, twirling it a few times, while silently counting his sheep to make sure none was missing.

A noise from behind startled him. Out of the corner of his eye he saw a yellow flash speed past him. The animals started to scatter as a mountain lion grabbed a lamb by the scruff of the neck and turned to carry its dinner back up the hill. Instantly the young boy dashed after the wild marauder. The sheep turned to watch the drama.

It so happened that Ishmael, a friend of David's father, was passing by and witnessed the drama. Immediately he reached into his robe, pulled out his mobile phone and speed-dialed his close friend. "Jesse, its Ishmael! I just saw a lion grab one of your sheep."

"What? Where is my son? He's supposed to be taking care of my flock."

"That's why I called you. Your son is chasing the lion now."

"Oh. You had me worried there for a minute."

"Jesse, he's going to get hurt. Oh . . . hold on!"

Ishmael was suddenly silent.

"What's going on?" Jesse shouted into his ear.

"Your son has attacked the lion. He's trying to pull the lamb out of its mouth. Jesse, I've got to stop him. That's too dangerous."

"No! Leave him alone!"

"Jesse, he's fighting the lion to save a worthless little lamb."

"Not worthless."

"But David could get killed. You don't want your son to die."

"Let him die! I sent David to take care of my sheep. That's what he is doing."

Let's pause here. **Certainly a responsible parent would never knowingly put his or her child in such danger. Would they?**

David is a man after God's heart. There is something more going on here. We don't know explicitly what Jesse's instructions were to David. But we do know how seriously David took his responsibility to care for the sheep.

Here's another thing. We know the Heavenly Father sent His Son to die for His sheep. Responsibility! Let Him die! Think about that for a minute in this context.

We return to our story. Ishmael said, "My dear Jesse, don't you think you are being a little reckless."

"Not at all."

Ishmael paused again, then said, "I don't believe it."

"What's happening?"

"Your son just pried the jaws of the lion off the lamb. The lamb is running away."

"All right, David! That's my boy!"

"I don't believe it! Jesse. He just killed the lion with his bare hands."

"See! There was no reason to worry. My son was doing his job."

FOR REFLECTION: *What responsibilities has God given you that seem dangerous? Are you willing to fulfill those responsibilities despite the danger or the pleas of those around you to stop?*

15

EVERY SHEEP IS PRECIOUS

> *"What man of you, having a hundred sheep, if he has lost one of them, does not leave the ninety-nine in the open country, and go after the one that is lost, until he finds it?" (Luke 15:4).*

Just what does it mean to be a man after God's heart? Let's continue to explore this question.

Jesus asked, If you have one hundred sheep and you lose one of them, isn't it natural to leave the ninety-nine to search for the lost one?

But the answer is no, that doesn't make any sense! Who will look after the ninety-nine sheep while the shepherd is off rescuing the one lost sheep? What if the shepherd slips and cracks open his head and then he can't rescue the runaway sheep and the ninety-nine are unprotected? Surely this is irresponsible!

Aren't there some other options? Can't the shepherd leave the ninety-nine with someone else and then go after the one? Jesus doesn't suggest this option. He *assumes* we will leave the ninety-nine and chase after the one. He would say we must act immediately—there is not a moment to lose.

I wonder how many of us would agree with Jesus' assumption? David would. Also Jesse, his father. Those sheep were David's responsibility. Not one of them was to be lost.

Besides, look at it from a sheep's point of view. The ninety-nine see the lion attack and carry off the lamb. They are afraid. They panic. Is there another lion lurking nearby ready to pick one of them off? They are about to scatter among the hills and rocks, irrationally seeking safety.

Then they see their shepherd. He's chasing after the lion. He pulls the lamb from the jaws of the attacker. Then he kills the lion. That animal will never terrorize these sheep again. Every sheep in the flock now recognizes an important truth. *If a wild animal attacks me, David will come to my rescue!*

That's the heart of Jesus for His Church.

That's the heart of Jesus for you and for me.

Further, that's the heart He expects each one of us to have for His sheep, especially for those who are persecuted for following Jesus in countries like North Korea and Iran and Pakistan and many other places around the world.

Do we care for the Father's sheep like that?

Many protest: That's dangerous, reckless. David could die!

True. That is the world in which God has placed us. **It is time to recognize something more important than our personal safety— God's call on our lives.** Without this experience of protecting sheep, David could never have faced Goliath and many other dangers that would follow his life.

As a father I have to wonder if Jesse ever considered the potential price of exposing his son to such danger. Would I be willing to let any of my five children face such risk? Indeed I have had to struggle with this question. It was one thing for me to travel behind the Iron Curtain or confront leaders of Hamas or Islamic Jihad. It was much harder to watch my children enter war zones in Afghanistan and Iraq and Uganda.

Yet my children belong to God, not me. David belonged to God, not Jesse. If Jesse had shielded his son from this danger, David would never have become the leader God needed for His people. He would never have confronted the giant and saved Israel.

Here we see why David was a man after God's heart. He was willing to die for his father's sheep. And his father was wise enough to let his son face that danger.

God so loved His sheep that He sent His Son to die for the sheep.

FOR REFLECTION: *Are you clinging to a false sense of security? How important is safety in your life? What will it take for you to let go and obey God's call on your life, even if it puts you at risk in some way?*

16

GOD'S CHOICE REVEALED

"Arise, anoint him, for this is he"
(1 Samuel 16:12).

Samuel has clear direction. This is the man—excuse me, the boy. Anoint him!

Samuel obeys, then quickly departs the scene.

David is standing in the midst of his brothers, probably wondering what is going on. Details are spare. There is no mention of the sacrifice—what about the heifer that Samuel had brought? There was no celebratory feast as there was at the anointing of Saul. It doesn't appear that Samuel explained what was happening to David.

I imagine everyone was a little confused. What did the seven older brothers think? You know they discussed it. "Why did Samuel honor David?" Wait a minute. Why is anyone anointed with oil by a prophet? One possibility—the high priest was anointed. However, the priest had to come from the tribe of Levi. No exceptions! That wasn't the explanation.

The other possibility was that David would become king. That didn't make sense either. Saul was king and his son Jonathan was next in line for the throne. It would seem that Jesse's family and all of Bethlehem witnessed this anointing but received no explanation for what had happened.

Now what? Samuel didn't stick around and that was probably a good idea. It was good that he hadn't announced God's purpose for this anointing. Word would certainly have reached Saul, and then Samuel and David and perhaps all of Bethlehem would have been in serious danger. All you have to do is leap forward a thousand years to see the possibilities. Three wise men (actually, we don't know how many, and were they really that wise?) traveled a great distance to ask King Herod where the next king of the Jews was living. With help from the religious leaders, Herod learned that the Messiah was to be born in Bethlehem. Then he proceeded to kill every male child two years of age and younger who lived in that region. It was a slaughter to protect his throne. Certainly Saul's later attempts to chase down David and kill him argue that Samuel's fears were justified.

So, what did David do? Did he ask his dad what this all meant? Probably Jesse didn't understand either. Meanwhile, the sheep were unattended. So David must have thought, *Better get back out there; take care of the flock; nothing has changed. When something changes, we will know.*

So David goes back to his regular, daily routine, back to tending sheep. Everyone in Bethlehem returns to their homes and jobs. Jesse's sons resume their lives—no doubt continuing to wonder, *What was that all about?* No one saw any immediate effect of the anointing.

There was one significant change, however. "The Spirit of the LORD rushed upon David from that day forward" (1 Samuel 16:13). **David was changed. He already had a heart after God. Now he also had power from God.** No one else saw it—yet. The revelation of God's hand on David would come soon enough.

Wait. Patience. Those are not welcome words for many of us. When we sense God's call, we want to act immediately. When we see an opportunity, we want to move out. Sometimes this is appropriate. In 1955 when I saw the brochure for the World Youth Congress in Poland, I knew I had to go. I didn't tell anyone—I just obeyed. However, at that time I didn't see the picture of ministry to the Persecuted Church. That understanding came later. (You can read about that in *God's Smuggler*.) I had no expectation, no plan, no burden, no dream. I didn't understand the significance of that trip—but God had launched me on the journey.

David had a glimpse that God's hand was on him. His brothers knew something was different. No one except Samuel had a clear picture of what was coming, and Samuel wasn't talking.

Therefore, since the way forward wasn't clear, David continued to fulfill his responsibility to his father. That's a good reminder for us. Sometimes the best way to serve God is simply to continue carrying out the responsibilities you already have. God will open the next door for you in His good time. David was standing by, ready to leap through the door when it opened. Are you standing by? Are you ready to spring into action the moment God calls?

> **FOR REFLECTION:** *Has God given you an assignment but it seems that the way forward is blocked? What is the vision or call? How can you prepare now for ministry when the opportunity comes? What is your responsibility as you wait?*

17

A LOOK UNDER THE HOOD

"The LORD sees not as man sees: man looks on the outward appearance, but the LORD looks on the heart" (1 Samuel 16:7).

Perhaps there really was an Ishmael, and he talked! (Don't remember Ishmael? Go back to devotion 14!)

Let's see what door opens for David. *Note*: David is a teenager, maybe sixteen years old. He's certainly not ready to be king. God will begin to prepare David by exposing him to the royal court. It won't be an official audience. He's not yet an advisor or cabinet minister. Rather, David will play a servant's role. That's all he was, really. There was an urgent need for a musician to play soothing music when King Saul was tormented by a harmful spirit sent by God. David didn't play his harp to entertain Saul and his court. He played soft music to soothe a troubled soul. The object was to calm King Saul, not to bring attention to David.

When the tormenting spirit left Saul and he was engrossed in his duties, David was dismissed. He went back home and returned to his regular job—caring for the sheep. The teenager didn't object. He never said, "Hey, I was just at the King's court. I'm not going back to those stupid, smelly sheep. I'm beyond that now!" No, David just did his job.

Again and again David was summoned to serve King Saul— we don't know how many times. Apparently at some point Saul noticed David. He liked the boy. He looked handsome and strong. "I'll make him an armor-bearer," he decreed. Saul already had several armor-bearers. This was no big deal to Saul. It was just a nice honor for a faithful servant.

Probably David realized that this wasn't the reason he had been anointed. Yet without more information all he could do was wait patiently, be a good shepherd, serve Saul faithfully, and so continue until more was revealed.

It's important here to realize David's qualifications for leadership. In the eyes of people around him, he had none! Sure, he was a good-looking lad. But there were thousands of such boys in Israel. It takes more than good looks and a little musical ability to become God's hero.

Realize that God can use anyone. That's the point! There is no obvious mold that identifies someone as a man or woman of God. You have to lift the hood and see what's underneath, and only God can do that.

Notice that David didn't blow his own trumpet. Until he faced King Saul and offered to fight Goliath, he probably never told anyone about slaying the bear and lion. David let his deeds speak for themselves. But who noticed? If you don't brag about your accomplishments, who will? Still David didn't boast. (Maybe he learned from hearing stories about Joseph, who bragged about his dreams to his older brothers. Slavery and jail time didn't appeal to David.) However, a servant who could influence Saul must have seen David.

A LOOK UNDER THE HOOD

God used that servant to report that David was a skillful musician, "a man of valor, a man of war" and more (1 Samuel 16:18). It was an impressive recommendation. Don't make too much of that, however. After all, how did he know David was a man of war? To date, David had never been to war.

What God sees is the potential of David. It began with the sheep. He was responsible even if it meant risking his life. Perhaps it also showed in the songs David played on the harp or composed during those quiet moments when the sheep were lying in the field and no wild animals threatened their safety. God could see into David's heart. He knew what the boy was thinking.

What does God see in you? Why does God choose any person to do His work? More specifically, why would He choose you?

Do you realize your potential? It doesn't matter if you have a great resume or none at all. The sky is the limit. It's up to you to make the most of your potential. You also have the power to destroy that potential by choosing not to obey God. That's what Saul did. So did David—later in his life he committed adultery and murder. What was the difference? Why did God's Spirit abandon Saul and send instead a tormenting spirit to him? Why was David still a man after God's heart? There was one huge difference. Saul never repented of his disobedience. When David was confronted with his sin, he immediately repented and threw himself on the mercy of God. God always accepts genuine repentance. You can view David's heart in Psalm 51.

When David did what was right, he never bragged about his accomplishments, not even about his victory over Goliath. Rather he trumpeted what God had done.

Take note of this because it's very important. **Who receives the glory in your life? Are you drawing attention to yourself? Or is**

your life a testimony to the greatness of God? If the latter, then someday you may have a chance to face off against a giant where victory is impossible—unless God acts!

FOR REFLECTION: *Is God receiving the glory in your life? What is the evidence?*

18

DAVID'S OPPORTUNITY IS KNOCKING

"Jesse said to David his son, 'Take for your brothers . . . these ten loaves. . . . Also take these ten cheeses to the commander of their thousand. See if your brothers are well'" (1 Samuel 17:17-18).

I believe in coincidences! We usually call it by other names—providence, God's will. Often nonbelievers say something is *luck*. Others protest that luck is not part of God's plan. My friend Johnny Mitchell used to say, "The more you pray, the more luck you have." God works through natural circumstances to put all the right pieces in place so that God's man will be in exactly the right place at the right moment.

It's time to move David from the sheep field to the battlefield. One day, not just any random day, Jesse gave David an assignment. (Who planted the thought in Jesse's mind?) Perhaps David arose that morning with nary an inkling that his life was about to change dramatically. He intended to go about his normal routine when Papa called him. "Here, take this grain and ten loaves of bread to your brothers. Also take these ten cheeses to their commander. See how your brothers are getting along and bring word back to me."

Before David carries out the assignment, he finds another shepherd to look after the sheep (v. 20). He doesn't realize this is the last time he has to worry about the flock. Then he travels to Elah Valley where the armies position themselves for a battle no one wants to fight. God's man is now in the right place to hear the giant's threats and become Israel's champion.

If you say yes to the Lord, you will always get to the right place at the right time. Just obey! Honestly, that's how I've tried to live life and as a result I've seen many miracles. Okay, I'm going to stop calling it luck or coincidence! One old story will illustrate my point. I told it in *God's Smuggler* but it bears repeating in this context.

It happened when I drove my Volkswagen beetle on my first trip to Yugoslavia in 1957. I had been given the name of a Christian leader in Zagreb. He had occasionally ordered Bibles from the Dutch Bible Society. However, they had not heard from him since the dictator Tito had taken control in 1945. Nevertheless I wrote the man a carefully worded letter stating that I would visit his country toward the end of March.

When I arrived in Zagreb, I hunted for his address, not knowing if my contact even lived there. Meanwhile several weeks earlier my letter had been delivered to this address. The tenant had no idea of the person's whereabouts and returned it to the post office. For two weeks a search was made for the man's address. (Isn't that in itself a miracle!) On the very day I entered Yugoslavia, the letter from this mysterious Dutchman was finally delivered. With only a vague sense that he should do something, the man boarded a tram and traveled across the city to his old apartment. The moment he arrived, I pulled up in my Volkswagen and stepped out on the curb, not two feet from him. The leader saw my license plates and guessed I was the Dutchman who had written to him.

What a joy it was to combine our stories and realize that God had brought us together. A coincidence some would say. I could tell you hundreds of similar stories. When do we stop calling it luck and admit that God just may be orchestrating great moments in our individual lives and in history?

Obedience to God: what an exciting way to live! You never know what will happen next. When you least expect it, God may bring you face-to-face with a giant that He intends for you to kill. You can't possibly do it, of course.

But let's not rush ahead of our story. It's time first to prepare for the battle.

FOR REFLECTION: *Do you believe in luck? How do you see God orchestrating the circumstances in your life?*

PART THREE

PREPARING FOR BATTLE

19

WHAT TO DO WITH THE WRONG MESSAGE

"Behold, the champion, the Philistine of Gath, Goliath by name, came up out of the ranks of the Philistines and spoke the same words as before. And David heard him" (1 Samuel 17:23).

Finally, we reach the battlefield. David is exactly where God wants him to be. But David doesn't understand yet what to do. How will he find out? How will he discern God's will?

David only knows he has the duty, which his father gave him, and he is determined to fulfill it. He arrives just as the Israelite army is moving into battle formation. They are shouting war cries, lining up in their ranks, heading to the frontline. This was not a good time to deliver presents to his brothers or their commander. So David is logical—store the goods with the one who manages supplies and go out with the crowd. Who knows what he might see.

David does what any eager boy would do. He goes through the crowd and finds his brothers. "Dad sent me with food," he reports.

"Great," says Eliab. "We're sick of army rations. Now, get out of our way. We've got a battle to fight."

Except, as we already know, there is no fight. Instead, guess who emerges—again. Here comes Goliath. For the first time David hears what the others have heard eighty times.

David can't control the giant's words. Neither can we avoid hearing the words of the enemy. He shouts his messages constantly through the media and Internet. However, we can filter those words through God's Word. We can be people of The Book.

What will David do with the words he hears? **David didn't know he was prepared for this moment, but he was.** He didn't try to argue with Goliath. Words were useless against the giant. Besides, Goliath's words were backed up by serious power. Argue with him and he'd squash you without a second thought.

But neither was David intimidated by the words of his brothers. Eliab spoke for them when he ridiculed David and told him to go back home and take care of that measly little flock of sheep. Intimidation is still a major tool the devil uses today. He shouts insults at Christians through the media and intimidation becomes humiliation. Those closest to us inform us that we can't do anything about it. We are worthless. We shouldn't even try. Resistance is futile.

We Christians may try to ignore the message, but that's virtually impossible. Some may respond with a negative message or recite biblical platitudes others don't believe and don't want to hear. Some demand that society adhere to a standard they no longer embrace. We may criticize those who try to make a difference—because their theology doesn't match ours, so we assume God could not possibly use them. Many Christians argue constantly about God and His ways. But their arguing makes me wonder, *Do they really know God?*

David knew God. That made all the difference in how he responded.

FOR REFLECTION: *What messages from the culture (for example, from television, publications, music, Internet) intimidate you? What lies is the enemy shouting at you? How can you resist those messages?*

20

A CONFRONTATION PHILOSOPHY

"All the men of Israel, when they saw the man, fled from him and were much afraid" (1 Samuel 17:24).

Fear immobilizes an entire army. Israel, God's chosen people, are powerless.

The people of Israel faced two enemies. One external, the other internal. The external enemy was obvious. Has there ever been a more imposing soldier than Goliath? His defenses were impregnable, his weapons awesome. Plus he was backed by an overpowering army.

The internal enemy was more devastating. The people cowered in fear. They were defeated before the fight. They had forgotten the promises of God. Where was the confidence of Joshua's armies when the Israelites conquered the land? This wasn't the peaceful, victorious, prosperous life that God clearly intended for His people.

It's a pattern that developed over time. The Philistines didn't suddenly appear. They had raided and intimidated the Israelites over many years. Israel was defeated long before Socoh. In fact I don't know why they even bothered to go to Socoh.

Why didn't David also flee in fear? David was courageous because he had a different perspective. **David didn't see a hopeless** situation; he knew this giant was no match for David's God. Further, David knew this God personally, which gave him the confidence his countrymen lacked.

Now I must make a critical point here. You can't confront every problem in society. You can't speak out against every wrong and injustice you see or hear about. Some people try—they attempt to be the conscience of a culture—but inevitably they fail. We need to know when to speak and when to be silent. David even prayed, "Set a guard, O Lord, over my mouth; keep watch over the door of my lips!" (Psalm 141:3).

We tend to speak too little about the really important things and make up for it by saying too much about trivial things. When we hear messages we know are wrong, we're afraid but often helpless to discern when to take action and when to leave a battle for God to fight another day. Not every fight is your fight. David chose the right battle to fight.

There were several reasons that David knew this was his battle. He knew that the words of Goliath were most certainly not of God. He saw the effect of Goliath's words on Israel—cowering in fear was not how God's people should behave. The Spirit of God was residing in David. And he knew God and therefore recognized when the Spirit was moving him to take action.

This was the moment for which God had prepared David. He knew it in his spirit.

Do you recognize the Holy Spirit's leading in your life? To do so, you have to get to know God, know His Word, and obey Him in the little things. Then when a big opportunity arises, you will recognize it as your moment. It is the giant God has called *you* to confront.

It won't be easy to respond. You probably won't feel prepared. David didn't have any experience in warfare. He certainly didn't know the end result. But he was a gambler. Spurred by God's Spirit, he boldly took action. It was an act of total faith in his great big God.

One of the first giants I had to confront was how to pay for two years of missionary college in Glasgow. There was no tuition, but I had to pay ninety pounds for room and board each year. That was a big figure for me in 1953. I had enough money from working at a chocolate factory to pay the first third when I arrived. That was it. I could expect nothing from my family and I had no means to earn any more money. I told God I would not go into debt. If He didn't provide what I needed for each payment on or before the day it was due, I would quit and go back to work in the factory.

I can testify that God never failed me. I never mentioned my needs to anyone. Gifts arrived from various people—none of them knew each other, and, except for Uncle Hoppy, gifts never came from the same people twice. The funds arrived just in time for me to make my required payments. It was always exactly what I needed, never more.[2] Yes, God delights in slaying giants for us. That experience made me realize my God was big enough to handle every challenge He put in my path.

FOR REFLECTION: *How big is your God? Why can you trust Him with the giants you face in your life?*

21

RIGHT AND WRONG MOTIVES

"And the men of Israel said, '. . . the king will enrich the man who kills [the giant] with great riches and will give him his daughter and make his father's house free in Israel'" (1 Samuel 17:25).

There was considerable material incentive for someone, anyone, to step forward and fight the giant. For that matter there was motivation for Saul to do it. If he fought Goliath, he could save himself from paying a big reward and losing some of his tax revenue.

We already know why Saul couldn't fight Goliath. The Spirit of God had departed from him. He knew he was defenseless. Still, it would seem that the prize package for this reality show ought to have had men lining up to fight.

- Great riches (one million dollars? That's not so much these days. Maybe ten million or more?)
- Marriage into the royal family (We don't know if Saul's daughter was pretty or smart. Maybe she wasn't such a prize after all.)
- No more taxes for his father's household for life (I can imagine a few fathers pushing their sons—"Get out there and fight like a man!")

Money, sex, and power—these are the rewards the world offers. Clearly these weren't enough to overcome the fears of Israel. And they aren't enough today. If you capture the illness of our time, you may think, *Anything for money, sex, and power.* See how people line up to buy lottery tickets when the jackpot rises to eight or nine figures. Winning won't ease their fears. Often it adds new fears. There are numerous stories of lottery winners losing everything.

Sex, unless in a marriage relationship, doesn't make people happy either. There's the fear of an unwanted pregnancy or contracting AIDS. And if you have power, there is always someone who wants to take it away from you. Saul sure was afraid of losing power once David became the people's champion.

Money, sex, and power are not enough motivation to risk your life for the Kingdom of God.

David challenged the motives of Israel's soldiers. He understood clearly what the rewards were—he asked several men to be sure—and apparently he found them insufficient because he never mentioned them again. So what was David's motivation? Listen: "Who is this uncircumcised Philistine, that he should defy the armies of the living God?" (v. 26). David appealed to the honor of God and God's people, but the soldiers didn't get it. The men repeated what they had already said: This is the reward Saul is offering. I believe they figured: *That's not a good enough reason to get myself killed.*

David, however, driven by the honor of God, found courage. He understood that Goliath had to be challenged. The reproach of Israel had to be removed. What would people think of God if the Philistine warrior won in a walkover? It was unthinkable that one man would crush an army. And to think that the Philistine god, Dagon, would be considered the supreme deity! That was totally unacceptable!

RIGHT AND WRONG MOTIVES

FOR REFLECTION: *Describe what brings honor to God in your life. Is there a giant challenging the honor of God in your life? What is that challenge?*

22

WHY DAVID HAD TO RESPOND

> *"Who is this uncircumcised Philistine, that he should defy the armies of the living God?"*
> *(1 Samuel 17:26).*

How did David know Goliath was uncircumcised? The words that came out of Goliath's mouth made it obvious. It was clear the giant was not a secret believer. There was no thought of trying to convert this pagan. Goliath defied the ranks of Israel, but in reality he was defying God. He was declaring that he was so great not even God could defeat him. Such blasphemy cannot go unchallenged.

David took the bait. "My God is plenty big enough to take down this infidel. In fact I'll prove it!" This response made God responsible. And David stated this clearly to King Saul: "The LORD who delivered me from the paw of the lion and from the paw of the bear will deliver me from the hand of this Philistine" (v. 37). David may have defeated lions and bears in hand-to-paw combat, but he knew who was responsible. God got the glory.

If there is any doubt, David repeats this as he confronts Goliath just before the fight is engaged. "This day the LORD will deliver you into my hand" (v. 46). And God accepts the responsibility. He will fight alongside David and it will be no contest. The giant will fall! The greater the giant, the greater the fall.

Now, that is not an open invitation for us to go fight every giant. Of course, some giants choose us. We can't run away when we learn a child has a drug addiction or the doctor tells us the diagnosis is cancer. Other times we must soberly realize the dangers and discern if this is the fight God would have you or me fight.

I can't help but think of my dear friend Corrie ten Boom. She told her story in *The Hiding Place*—about how her family hid Jews during World War II. They knew the risks and fought the giant anyway. They were caught and sent to a concentration camp. Corrie survived. Her father and sister, Betsie, died in the camp.

Many years later, after Corrie had traveled the world telling her story and challenging people to follow Jesus, she came home to "retire." For the first time she bought a house in Haarlem, just a few kilometers from where her family used to live and hide Jews. She settled down to make her home. One day I visited her and admired the comfortable furnishings, the magnificent family clocks her father had repaired, and the beautiful garden. Pointing to her garden I said, "Corrie, God is good to you."

Quickly and forcefully Corrie replied, "God was also good when Betsie died. God is *always* good!"

You may not have to fight a particular battle today. That doesn't mean you won't have to fight the next battle. And there may be casualties. That's the reason discernment is critical. What battle has God called you to fight? The ten Boom family knew God required them to protect Jews. Corrie survived, but her father and sister paid with their lives.

Consider this question as you hear God calling you to battle: **If I fight this battle am I willing to die?**

A friend of mine told me about how he and his wife were invited to go on a short mission to a dangerous Islamic country where there was a lot of upheaval. The couple knew God had called them to this work. Family and friends protested, however, that it was too dangerous. Better to wait for another time when it was calmer.

The husband and wife were not swayed. They had a heartfelt conversation. Were they willing to die while on this mission if that is what God allowed? The man told me their conclusion: "One thing I know is that, unless the Lord returns soon, I will die someday. My prayer is that my death will bring glory to God. I will only die once, so I've told God I want my death to be in a manner that will bring Him the most glory. My wife joins me in that conviction."

I share their passion. God has spared my life many times—probably more times than I realize. I could go boldly to many dangerous places because all I did was follow God's lead. Now (as I write this) I'm eighty-four. My time is short. What will bring God the most glory as I live my final days in service to Him? This is my desire: **Whether I live or die, to God be the glory.**

This was David's passion as well. Still, he was confident—maybe because of his anointing by Samuel—that he had many years ahead of him. So he took the risk. He stepped forward to fight the giant.

FOR REFLECTION: *How do you respond to my friend's statement that he wants his death to be in a manner that brings God the most glory?*

23

FAMILY BACKLASH

"Eliab's anger was kindled against David"
(1 Samuel 17:28).

Don't expect your family to support you when you confront a giant. If they do, that's a bonus. It's nice to have their support, but if God has called you, you don't need their permission or blessing. If God has chosen you for a dangerous assignment, then He is sufficient to meet your needs, even if there is no one else standing with you.

Still we long for the backing of family and it hurts when they don't respond. David's brothers were certainly not his fans. They made no attempt to build David's self-esteem. Fortunately he didn't need it.

Eliab spoke what Abinadab and Shammah were probably thinking. Their four younger brothers would likely have supported Eliab had they also been on the scene. Just what was Eliab's problem? Jealousy, perhaps. Seeing his kid brother interact with the soldiers irritated him. Who did David think he was? I can almost hear Eliab's cynical thoughts: *Listen to that twerp.* "What shall be done for the man who kills this Philistine and takes away the reproach from Israel?" *They've just told him the reward but he keeps on asking. He probably imagines himself becoming some sort of superhero.*

Finally, Eliab could stand it no longer. He exploded with anger. "What are you doing here anyway? Go home and take care of your stupid sheep." Funny, then Eliab says that he knows what is in David's heart! That's right. He thinks David is filled with pride and evil thoughts. "You just want to see the battle."

No, David wants to *fight* the battle!

Obviously Eliab had no idea what was in David's heart. But the jealousy, anger, prejudice, and pride in Eliab's heart warped the oldest brother's perspective. David could do nothing right. *What does he know? I'm a grown man, a soldier. He's just a runny-nosed kid.*

David shows a flash of frustration. "What's your problem?" is in essence his response to his brother. Then he ignores Eliab and continues talking with the soldiers.

Oh my, how many families can relate to these dynamics? Maybe you don't have such antagonism at home. Perhaps the resistance you feel is more subtle. It's couched in phrases like, "You can't do that! It's not safe." Families say things like, "Don't take the Gospel to that Islamic country. You might get hurt. You might get killed. Think of your spouse, your kids. Stay where it's safe."

Give your family the benefit of the doubt. They mean well. The concern is genuine.

Facing giants is dangerous. Your job, however, is not to win them over. **David is more concerned with what God commands than what his brothers think or his own safety. That should be our attitude as well.**

Jesus commands his followers to GO into all the world and make disciples. He doesn't promise that all who go will come back. Friends and family will protest and explain that this command doesn't mean *you* have to go into danger. They are scared. Well, so are you. You go anyway. You obey God anyway. Your conduct and the faithfulness of God, not your arguments, have to win them over.

FAMILY BACKLASH

Before we leave this scene, let's jump forward a few chapters. David has defeated Goliath. He's won many additional battles. Saul is now chasing him. What does his family do? First Samuel 22 tells us David is hiding in the cave of Adullam. His brothers and all of his father's house decide to travel to the cave and join him. The tables have turned. With a jealous king it probably wasn't safe for Jesse or his sons to stay any longer in Bethlehem. Where did they go for protection? To the youngest, to the one who was filled with God's Spirit, to the one who in God's strength could defeat giants and Philistine armies.

David didn't have to defend himself against his big brother. God took care of that.

FOR REFLECTION: *In what ways have you allowed, or are you allowing, your family and friends to hold you back from what the Lord is calling you to do?*

24

GOD OPENS THE DOOR

"When the words that David spoke were heard, they repeated them before Saul, and he sent for him" (1 Samuel 17:31).

David has stirred up the troops. After Israel has endured weeks of abuse from the giant, at last someone is acting without fear. Words are powerful. We've seen the power of Goliath's message. Now we glimpse the charisma of a passionate teenager. He's saying, "This situation is not right! This Philistine is insulting the armies of the living God. We don't have to stand around and take it. Let's do something!" David is essentially asking: "Isn't anyone going to stand up to this giant? If no one steps up, then I will!"

I don't know whether the soldiers believed David had the solution but they had sure heard enough from the Philistine. They needed good news. If this boy had an answer, then Saul needed to know it. Someone reported what was going on, and David was brought before the one with authority to act.

Notice that David didn't march up to the king and demand an audience. He didn't pull rank and tell Saul's chief of staff, "I'm the king's armor-bearer. You have to get me an appointment." **It's not up to us to manipulate our way into places of power and**

influence. If we are faithful to follow God and His ways, then in His time He opens up the opportunity. God arranged this meeting for David.

Another important point is that David followed the chain of command. No doubt he was becoming convinced he should take on the Philistine but he didn't go out and fight the giant before going through the established authority of the king. Of course, King Saul could have said no! Though really he had no choice. By getting the backing of the king, David now had the entire community behind him. This is vital. Solo acts rarely achieve much. We need a pioneer to show the way—to open up the possibilities, but people need to come behind the pioneer if there is to be a movement. For that you need the authority of leadership. When David went out to confront Goliath, he had the entire army (praying for him, no doubt) ready to act when the outcome became clear.

When you feel called to do something for God, recognize the opportunities and then get the backing of proper authority. Now I'll admit I wasn't very good at that early in my missionary ventures. I went to Poland in 1955 and told no one. But when I came back, I began to report to churches and other meetings what God was doing. I told them about the need of the Church behind the Iron Curtain, and the opportunities to meet that need. In time a few men and women joined me and we gained prayer support and financial assistance. I still had the pioneer spirit but God didn't let me do it alone.

Faithfulness leads to opportunity. David's adventure in Socoh didn't happen by chance. God brought all the pieces together. David recognized that God had put him there for this moment, not as an observer but as a leader, a leader who would have to fight.

One more thing. David respected Saul's authority but he wasn't impressed by it. The trappings of royalty—the banners, the medals, the entourage—can blur our perspective. But David wasn't impressed or intimidated by power. He proclaimed God's word even to the king.

> FOR REFLECTION: *Do you seek influential roles for the purpose of gaining power or to bring God glory? How do the two approaches differ?*

25

A CRAZY IDEA

"David said to Saul, '... your servant will go and fight with this Philistine'" (1 Samuel 17:32).

So David stood before King Saul. "Don't you worry anymore," he said. "I'll fight the giant."

What a bold (stupid?) statement to make. Such confidence! Does David even know what he is saying? I'm not sure he does. He's acting under compulsion of the Spirit. He's defending the honor of God. He knows something must be done and if no one else steps forward, he concludes that God must have called him to do the job.

Is he crazy? David has no weapons with which to fight the giant. What is he thinking? David is confident but not in himself. His confidence is in God. He believes God has prepared him for this conflict. Therefore God will use him as he is—a shepherd. The way God called him is the way God will use him.

Too many people feel God can't use them as they are. They are convinced they have to get a certain degree and know influential people and have a decent sized bank account, and a certain title after their name (Ph.D., CEO, Chief something) wouldn't hurt. Only then will God use them. But those things mean nothing. There is always someone with a more prestigious degree or a fatter Rolodex or a bigger bank account or a fancier title.

Besides, the moment you are conscious of your abilities, it becomes unlikely that God will get the credit.

David was not awed with the trappings of power nor was he swayed by outward appearances. The size of the man, big or small, made no difference. Perhaps a plan had already started to form in his mind. He may have been thinking, *the bigger the man, the bigger the target.* Goliath can either scare you as he did all the Israelites. Or you can think, *he's so big I can't miss!* Maybe David was thinking about all the years he'd practiced with the sling. He'd chased off many a wild animal slinging stones with great accuracy. Big or small made no difference. Just one stone had to get through a hole in Goliath's helmet. That was the giant's weak spot. And such a big target—*really, I can't miss!*

David revealed none of these thoughts. Naturally Saul was not so sure. Logic must have told him this was madness. *Look at this scrawny kid. He has no armor. He has no weapons. He has no training.* Saul also had no memory. He may have thought he had seen this kid somewhere else but he couldn't place him. He didn't remember that a year or two before, a servant had told him about this shepherd who was "a man of war." He didn't remember that David played soothing music for him and that David was one of his armor-bearers—how many did he have anyway? He certainly wasn't paying attention to the fact that God's Spirit was in David.

Of course, David must eventually make a case that he is indeed the person to fight Goliath. Saul rightly notes the downsides of the idea: you're just a kid and Goliath is a trained warrior. David is a person of humility but here he has to reveal that he has fought and defeated the lion and the bear. "This uncircumcised Philistine shall be like one of them" (v. 36). Why? Not because David is Goliath's equal. Not because his earlier experience guaranteed success. No, David makes Saul understand the reason: "He has defied the armies of the living God." That's the reason David has to fight him.

Then David hammered home the point. It's not about me. It's about God. "The LORD who delivered me from the paw of the lion and from the paw of the bear will deliver me from the hand of this Philistine" (v. 37). Faith radiates with a minimum of words. This is the powerful witness of the Spirit. David's testimony and proclamation are a powerful combination. They gave David confidence and inspired King Saul. David had elevated the battle to a spiritual level and made it God's cause.

This argument gets through to Saul. The king had known the power of God earlier in his reign. He's lost that power but he recognized it in the teenager. So he thought, *Maybe, just maybe this will work. It's crazy, but what other options do I have?*

"Go," ordered Saul, "and the LORD be with you!"

The one who has dismissed God in his own life is now totally depending on God to rescue him and his army through a teenage boy.

FOR REFLECTION: ***How do you take the focus off your own abilities and remain humble, trusting only in God's abilities?***

26

A FEEBLE ATTEMPT TO HELP GOD

"Then Saul clothed David with his armor"
(1 Samuel 17:38).

Saul was thinking: *Okay, it's decided. David convinced me. I don't know why exactly. Something in his confidence—more like cockiness—makes me want to believe he will succeed.*

Then Saul thought a little more: *This is a crazy idea. What was I thinking? I'm taking a terrible risk. It can't possibly succeed. I could change my mind but then I'll look weak. I just made a decision, probably a stupid decision. But it's done. I can't go back on my word now.*

So what shall I do? The kid has no armor, no weapon. He's defenseless. The giant will eat him up and spit out the bones. I can't let him go like this. I must do something to help him. There's no time to put him through boot camp. An hour's worth of sword drills won't make up for the Philistine's years of training.

I've got it. The least I can do is provide him with a little protection. I'll lend him my armor. Maybe he can withstand the first blow of the spear. He might be able to parry a swipe of the giant's sword. He will still get killed. But at least I can say I did all I could. Then it's not my fault.

Of course, we don't really know what Saul was thinking. The

above paragraphs are just speculation. We do know that he lent David his armor. David—perhaps he still didn't know his plan of battle or he was just being polite to the king—graciously accepted. The picture now becomes rather humorous. The roles are reversed. The soldier becomes the armor-bearer, and armor-bearer the soldier. Piece by piece Saul dresses the boy. First, a helmet of bronze goes on David's head. It's rather loose. David turns his head but the helmet stays put. If he's to wear this helmet into battle, he must keep his eyes fixed straight ahead or somehow tighten the fit with a chin strap.

Next comes the coat of mail. It's beautiful—strong, light, and extra, extra large on David's medium frame. The coat of mail droops over his knees.

"Here's my sword," says Saul. David straps it on over the armor that covers his waist. It's a long sword and scrapes along the ground as he takes a step. Maybe if he moved it up—to chest level.

"Walk around a bit," says the king. "How does it feel?"

Ridiculous is how it feels. David tries. He takes a few steps. The armor jiggles around him. Already it starts to feel heavy and hot. He can barely move.

"I'm sorry, your majesty, but this won't work. Thank you very much, but I haven't had a chance to use these and get used to them." David doesn't mention that the armor doesn't fit—that's rather obvious. Saul can't argue. At least he tried.

Now a plan becomes clearer in David's mind. The Spirit is stirring within. Who is this young man? A shepherd. What does he have? A staff. A pouch. A sling. Plus quickness. *That big giant can't move like I can.* **David will stay true to who he is and fight as a shepherd, just as he fought the lion and bear.** But God will have to protect him and give him the victory, for one thing is very clear. To have any chance of victory he will have to get close. He will have one shot, two at the most, and then the giant will be on top of him.

Did David feel any fear at that point? Or did adrenaline surge and the excitement of this adventure kick in? Perhaps he was thinking, *Wow, God, I can't wait to see how you deliver me out of this mess!*

FOR REFLECTION: **David fought Goliath as a shepherd facing a wild beast. What skills and experiences do you have that God might use when you engage in battle?**

PART FOUR

THE BATTLE

27

AN ARSENAL OF FIVE STONES

"Then he took his staff in his hand and chose five smooth stones from the brook and put them in his shepherd's pouch" (1 Samuel 17:40).

What's that kid doing by the stream?

Picture the scene. Two armies facing each other across a valley. To engage, each army would have to rush down a steep slope, carefully step over stones, and wade through the stream. Those rocks would be slippery, not the best footing for a soldier. That's one reason David needed his staff—to provide balance as he stepped over the rocks.

Goliath, lounging on a patch of grass on the other side of the brook, watched. He was curious. During the forty days he'd issued his challenge, no one had come down the slope into the valley. Now here was this boy, dressed in a simple short robe and wearing sandals. There was a pouch around his waist. He was carrying a staff. He was bending over and picking up stones.

There was no threat here. *Stupid kid! He's oblivious. Must be mentally challenged. Doesn't he realize there's a war going on here? Isn't he afraid of the big bad giant? He should be. But he doesn't pay me any attention.*

The kid put the stones in his pouch and looked up at the giant, stared at him. The giant was perplexed. *Surely . . . no, it's not possible. They would never send a boy to do a man's job. Someone's playing a joke. Very funny those Israelites.*

Carefully David stepped on the slick rocks as he made his way across the creek. Then he stood and faced the Philistine on the enemy side of the stream. Goliath sat up. Was the boy going to throw a rock at him? Then he saw David reach into his pouch and pull out a sling.

Was Goliath taking David seriously? Not at all! But he was cautious. He was a trained fighter. He couldn't afford to let his guard down. This could be a trick. The boy could be a decoy to allow the real opponent to sneak around behind him.

So, we've reached the climax of our story. The battle is about to begin. First, however, each side must have his say. We must clearly understand the stakes. Before a "shot" is fired, Goliath and David will each reveal his true character.

Do you know why you are facing your giant? Why are you in the battle? Why are you taking a risk? Isn't life about being safe and secure? That's what most of us strive for.

Not David. He was facing the giant all alone with no protection. Did he realize the implications? Maybe as he looked up at nine-and-a-half feet of muscle, he began to rethink his stand. No! David was committed and soon we will understand why.

FOR REFLECTION: *Think about the battle you are facing. Are you ready to take the risk involved? Are you committed to fight until the end?*

28

THE ENEMY SPEAKS

*"He looked David over and saw that
he was only a boy . . . and he despised him"
(1 Samuel 17:42, NIV).*

The giant now realized that David really was Israel's champion. Before the contest there was trash talk. Goliath shouted first. Everyone on both sides of the valley watched and listened. The voices of the two combatants carried and reverberated off the rocks.

"Am I a dog?" shouted Goliath. (In the margin of my Bible I've written, "Yes!")

"Am I a dog, that you come to me with sticks?" (v. 43). David was carrying one stick—his shepherd staff. Maybe the giant's vision was not good.

Then Goliath, his booming, guttural voice filling the valley, cursed David by his gods. When a man has lost control of a situation he often resorts to swearing, plus intimidation: "Come to me, and I will give your flesh to the birds of the air and to the beasts of the field" (v. 44).

Either the giant was very cocky or he covered up his anxiety with strong words that he believed would instill fear in his opponent or both. I don't think Goliath had any apprehension. He was super confident that his size, strength, armor, and overwhelming weaponry were no match for this kid. He would crush the boy and feed him to the vultures. The Philistine army would impose their will on the obstinate Israelites and make them pay for the insult of not properly responding to their champion's challenge.

Now we know the thinking of David's opponent:

- He clearly hates God.
- He is utterly confident in his own strength and ability.
- He supports his own (false) gods. Whether he really believes in them and worships them is another matter.

What Goliath doesn't realize, never even considers, is that he is a puppet. He and the whole Philistine army are agents of Satan but they don't know it. Goliath is only the mouthpiece for the real and mortal enemy. Satan intends to crush David and thwart God's plans for Israel.

Be careful not to jump to conclusions about giants today. Some would call Islam the Goliath of our age and insist that it must be defeated by argument and force. You probably know what I think—for me Islam means "I Sincerely Love All Muslims." People debate with me about this. I explain that Muslims do not hate Jesus. To them Jesus is the second greatest prophet. It's true that they hate the cross, the atonement, the blood, the resurrection. They hate all that the Son of God stands for. They hate when they hear us say that Jesus is the Son of God. That is the deeper reason why they resist Christians. We say Jesus is divine, which is a blasphemous statement to Muslims.

However, do Muslims *see* Jesus in us—in you, in me? Think about why Goliath mocked Israel. Pure and simple, it was because he didn't see God in Israel. **If God's people had been really living as God intended them to live, the Philistine army would realize**

they were fighting God and be rightly terrified.

Why do (some) Muslims hate Christians? Because they don't see the evidence of God at work in us. They mock us for that. They point to our culture—our movies, TV shows, books, music, and cartoons—and conclude that Muslims are holier than Christians because that's the logical conclusion to draw. They don't openly allow such filth in their culture.

We may protest and claim we live in a secular society. Muslims don't separate sacred and secular. To them faith, culture, and politics form one total system. We won't win that argument.

So, it's David's turn to respond. How does he answer Goliath's tirade?

FOR REFLECTION: *What is the evidence that Jesus is alive and at work in your life?*

29

DAVID RESPONDS

> *"Then David said to the Philistine,*
> *'You come to me with a sword and with a spear*
> *and with a javelin, but I come to you in the*
> *name of the* LORD *of hosts'" (1 Samuel 17:45).*

David isn't concerned with political correctness. He proclaims the truth and doesn't care who hears him. First, he states the obvious: "You come to me with a sword and with a spear and with a javelin." David acknowledges the superior weaponry of the Philistine. "But I . . ." David doesn't bother declaring his weapons but rather proclaims his authority in this confrontation: "I come to you in the name of the LORD of hosts, the God of the armies of Israel, whom you have defied. This day the LORD will deliver you into my hand" (vv. 45–46).

David is both a soldier and a prophet. Under the power of the Holy Spirit, he proclaims that God is God. David never considers negotiation—there is nothing to negotiate with the enemy who defies God. David is not interested in an ecumenical movement. That was a large part of Israel's problem—they thought pagan cultures and foreign religions could coexist in a nation under one God.

There is something powerful when a situation is so clearly black and white. In this day we have developed an appetite for compromise, for tolerance, for ecumenism. All points of view are valid. This syncretism plays more of a role in our churches than we realize. Without consciously thinking about it, many Christians accept that all roads lead to God.

Jesus says, "I am the way." Modern "experts" say, "That can't be right. That's your truth but not my truth. You can't impose your truth on me."

Well, David is about to impose The Truth on Goliath. He begins by declaring The Truth.

David is terribly bold. Why are we so timid? Because people will accuse us of being intolerant? Are we afraid of the possible consequences? David doesn't care. He must state what to him is obvious. This may seem risky. What if . . . ? What if God doesn't come through? What if David loses this fight?

No, this is not a risk! David knows exactly what he is doing. Any Israelite could have done the same. **Each Hebrew had the right to live in utter dependence on God. But they didn't trust Him like David did.** They didn't really know God. If they had spent less time cowering in fear and more time in their Scriptures, they would have understood the faithfulness God had shown to Abraham and Joseph and Moses. They should have spent the hours between Goliath's morning and evening insults immersed in the book of Joshua to see how God fought for them and drove the pagans out of the land.

I'm impressed today with how some brethren in the Persecuted Church understand this truth. For them there is no dialogue or cooperation with their oppressors. Their choice is simple: proclamation and imprisonment. As you can see—that's really no choice! The church in Russia and China has gone through great tribulations. In the process they settled this issue. They simply would not stay silent about Jesus. Whereas we in the free world, well, too many hardly acknowledge they know Him. The Persecuted Church shows us how to live by faith in the midst of spiritual war. That's why I believe the Persecuted Church is the church of the future. In fact it may be the only genuine church in the world today.

David knew The Truth. David declared The Truth. Then David acted on The Truth. Therefore David could confidently declare the outcome of this confrontation.

FOR REFLECTION: *How do you know and act on The Truth? What authority does this give you as you confront your giant?*

30

THE REASON FOR THE BATTLE

> *"This day the* LORD *will deliver you into my hand, and I will strike you down and cut off your head"*
> *(1 Samuel 17:46).*

Did David really understand the situation? I mean he was really too young to know systematic theology and doctrines of spiritual conflict. Clearly he was not quoting Scripture when he shouted to the Philistine.

Remember David is under the influence of the Holy Spirit. When you are Spirit-controlled and proclaim the Word of God under His power, there is a lot of liberty to say what you want. I'm not suggesting you make things up. I'm saying that the Gospel should be such a part of our lives that when we speak, we speak the truth of the Gospel, however we may articulate it.

Paul the Apostle says, "If you confess with your mouth that Jesus is Lord [declaration, proclamation] and believe in your heart that God raised him from the dead, you will be saved" (Romans 10:9). We must never water down the Gospel. David believed with his whole heart what God revealed in Scripture. He declared what he knew. Then he expected God to save him.

This is not how we fight war today. On a human level when two countries are at war, their diplomats behind the scenes seek a solution. Often there is some give and take. This situation in Elah Valley was very different. Ultimately David versus Goliath was a spiritual battle. **Here we have the forces of hell against God. God's honor is at stake.** You don't strike deals with the enemies of God.

We are in a mess today because we compromise with the enemy rather than trust God and what He has promised. Too many people are Christians on Sunday (or part of Sunday), but God has little or no part of their lives the rest of the week.

David seems to get a little carried away in his declaration. He promises to strike down Goliath and cut off his head. Then "I will give the dead bodies of the host of the Philistines this day to the birds of the air and to the wild beasts of the earth" (v. 46). Whoa, wait a minute! The deal was that the army of the loser serve the army of the victor. David has exceeded his authority. No one said anything about one army slaughtering the other. He's just committed Israel to war.

That's correct because David knew the nation's rights. These pagans had no right being in Israel. Their gods could never coexist with Israel's God. Compromise was not an option, only total victory, by God, and for God and His people. The Philistines should have been annihilated two hundred or more years earlier. They weren't. So David has started a fight that God approves.

By now it should be clear that David is not fighting for a reward. We never even hear that he claimed the prize for his victory. Those rewards were infinitely small compared to the single big issue. David is fighting with the right motive. He wants to bear witness.

Listen: "That all the earth may know that there is a God in Israel" (v. 46). Come on David, isn't that hyperbole? No, the whole earth *does* know. It's right there in the Bible. The story has been told and retold in picture books and storybooks and movies. David continues: "that all this assembly may know that the LORD saves not with sword and spear" (v. 47). Well, Israel has no spear and only two swords. This battle is designed for the people of God to witness the power of their God. Finally, "For the battle is the LORD's, and he will give you into our hand."

So, there it is. Let the battle begin!

FOR REFLECTION: *What is the evidence that you/we are engaged in spiritual battle? What witness do you bring to this battle?*

31

TO THE DEATH

"David ran quickly toward the battle line to meet the Philistine" (1 Samuel 17:48).

Goliath was angry. Finally, he realized the kid really intended to fight him. He got up and lumbered toward David. He couldn't move very quickly. He was huge, bulky, and carrying a couple hundred pounds of equipment.

David was limber, quick. He *ran* to the battle.

If this story were novelized, it would be a very short book. This is not a made-for-television special. If it were, there would be far more drama—ninety minutes at least with commercials. Many years ago Al recalls seeing a movie of the Bible that included this battle. David dodged and feinted. Goliath swung his sword and missed. David shot a stone and it clanged off the giant's armor. Goliath took another swipe and David skipped out of harm's way. How long did the scene last? I can assure you that the movie version took a lot longer than the actual battle.

David ran toward the giant. No trickery here.

David reached into his shepherd's bag and pulled out a stone. Deftly he loaded his sling. As he got closer, he whirled the sling furiously. Goliath never got a chance to use his superior strength because David let fly with the stone. It was a perfect shot smack in the middle of the giant's forehead. The stone found a welcome and empty head!

Goliath didn't know what hit him. Like a giant tree, he slowly starts to fall, picks up speed, and lands face first on the ground.

David doesn't have a moment to waste. There is no time for a celebration because the giant isn't dead—not yet.

David promised to cut off the Philistine's head. He has no sword, but the giant does. It is still in its sheath. David pulls out the sword and delivers the mortal thrust into the neck. Then he finishes the job, sawing the head from the body.

Still no time to celebrate. There remained an army to destroy. By removing the head of Goliath David had also chopped off the head of the Philistine army. Like a headless body, the army goes into convulsions. Trained soldiers panic and flee. Some drop their weapons—Israel re-armed that day. As the Israelite army pursues the enemy, it is a slaughter. Bodies are strewn from Socoh to the gates of Ekron and Gath, the main Philistine cities. Then the Hebrew soldiers take their time stripping the armor and swords off their fallen enemies. Next time there's an attack on the nation, they would be armed and ready.

There's one interesting observation we should make. It appears that something important is missing from this story. There is no prayer service before the battle. Saul doesn't call a prayer meeting. David doesn't request of his friends: "Pray for me." Given the significance of this event, we might expect to see that detail recorded. Isn't that curious? Not really. Prayer is not the habit of a backslidden nation. Maybe that was the first activity they dropped. No wonder they were so afraid.

I think another reason prayer isn't mentioned is because David obeys God and runs quickly to the challenge, trusting in God. The pious may insist we pray first. Fine. Pray! David is a man of prayer—read the Psalms; he wrote half of them. But here David realizes that it's time to ACT, to FIGHT. This is not the time for a prayer meeting but for action.

Never substitute prayer for obedience!

Of course, I believe in prayer—it's always been central to our work and ministry. But when God sends you on a mission, GO!

I need to add that David was prepared to go. There was no deceit in him—that was his secret. Too many Christians lead double lives—pious on the outside, rotten on the inside. If that describes you, then you will fail when you confront the giant. David succeeded because he lived a life of devotion to God. It was daily. His communion with God was often in solitude. So when God called him to take action, he was ready.

You know the results. Now you also know the reason for those results.

FOR REFLECTION: *What lessons do you take away from David's battle with Goliath that apply to your life and the spiritual battles you face?*

PART FIVE

AFTER THE BATTLE

32

LESSONS FROM THE BATTLEFIELD

*"So David prevailed over the Philistine. . . .
And the men of Israel and Judah rose with a shout
and pursued the Philistines as far as Gath and
the gates of Ekron" (1 Samuel 17:50, 52).*

The overpowering advantage of the Philistine military machine does them no good. **The Word of God, proclaimed by God's servant, is more powerful than all the resources of the enemy.**

As the Philistines flee before the suddenly energized forces of Saul, what are the enemy soldiers thinking? *I can't believe that a small boy is greater than our biggest and strongest warrior. Who is this God of Israel? Maybe this God really is greater.*

David's guts have provided God with a glorious display of His power. My, how we need to see more of that power today! Honestly how much power does the world see in our churches? I'm not talking about the trappings of power—prestige, political access, property, big buildings, large bank accounts.

I think it starts with righteous anger. Yes, Christians should become angry. "Be angry and do not sin" Paul writes (Ephesians 4:26). David was angry at the ineptness of Israel's army and Goliath's defiance of God. He was angry that no one stood up for the honor of God's name. With his response David displayed righteous anger. The verse in Ephesians ends by saying, "Do not let the sun go down on your anger." David didn't!

In light of Christ's work on the cross, righteous anger should lead to forgiveness of those who have wronged us, even if the persecutors don't ask for forgiveness. We serve a God who offers forgiveness. In the book of Jonah God sent a most reluctant prophet to Nineveh, the heart of Israel's worst enemy of the time, and the result was one of the biggest revivals of history.[3] At least one hundred and twenty thousand people repented, and God spared the city. The challenge today is to take the good news of God's forgiveness to our "enemies" so that they can have the chance to experience forgiveness just as God has forgiven us.

Allow me to give a personal illustration. In 2006 I was involved in a high level dialogue between Christians and Muslims in Tehran, Iran. The high level delegation of Christians was composed of a group of scholars and one "smuggler." I couldn't compete intellectually with the Muslim or Christian scholars, but I saw an opportunity to present the ayatollahs and other religious leaders with some good news.

It so happened that 2006 was the 400th anniversary of the artist Rembrandt's birth and there was a great deal of interest in the famous Dutch artist in Iran. So when my turn came to speak at this dialogue, I presented the leader of the Muslim delegation with a special Rembrandt Bible that contained beautiful full-color plates of the Dutch painter's religious paintings. One of the famous paintings is "The Raising of the Cross." I opened the Bible to that painting, which showed the soldiers lifting the cross in order to drop it upright into a hole.

The soldiers were dressed in Turkish dress—that was all Rembrandt knew of the Middle East look. But in the middle of the picture was a boy, dressed in the modern Dutch dress of that period, reaching out and touching the cross. That boy, I explained, was Rembrandt himself. The artist had inserted himself into the painting, saying in essence, "I identify with the one you are crucifying. He died for me!"

Here was the point I made to the Muslim scholars. A Christian is one who identifies with the death and resurrection of Jesus. I realize that's considered a blasphemous teaching in Islam, but they did not interrupt me. So I continued: "It is our failure to identify with Jesus in His crucifixion and resurrection and in obedience to His command to go into all the world and make disciples that is causing all the problems we face today in the world. I wish I could speak for the whole church worldwide. I cannot. I can only speak for myself when I ask for forgiveness because we did not identify with Jesus by visiting you Muslims. We did not reach out to you. We did not present Christ to you."

After that meeting, one of the leaders approached me and thanked me for "showing your heart." My point in sharing this was not that I was angry at the Muslims. I was angry at us Christians for having committed the sin of neglect. How could we blame them for the sin of terrorism when we had not been obedient to God's clear commands? We have not gone into all the world, we have not made disciples of all nations. We sent our merchants and soldiers into all the world, but not our missionaries. So now we are reaping the harvest.

Have we learned the lesson yet?

FOR REFLECTION: *When you look at the world around you, what makes you angry? What lessons from the battlefield might apply to how you respond to what you see?*

33

BACK WHERE THEY BELONG

"The people of Israel came back from chasing the Philistines, and they plundered their camp"
(1 Samuel 17:53).

Once the giant was dead, Israel drove the Philistines off their land and back to their own cities. Good! The enemy is back where they belong. They should have been driven out of the land long ago. Then Saul's army backs off and they plunder the Philistine camp. Well, that's good too. They finally arm themselves with proper weapons.

I wonder though if they should have stayed more focused on their counterattack. They didn't really finish the job. Before long the Philistines were able to regroup and they continued to plague Israel for many more years. What if Israel had decided enough is enough, laid siege to Gath and Ekron and the other Philistine cities, and determined that these pagans would never again be a threat to God's people? **This story has always been interesting and entertaining, but it should be much more than that. It should challenge our lives.** And this leads to another issue—Israel's weak leadership. Because of this they weren't able to entertain the war option. Listen to Saul talking to Abner, the commander of his army, "Whose son is this youth?" (1 Samuel 17:55). Saul's question should have been: "Who is the God of this youth?" And a follow-up question would be, "How do we find out God's will regarding the problem of the Philistines?"

Saul learned soon enough that Jesse was David's father. David himself revealed that. But Abner and the king and all the leaders around them should have immediately begun a process of revival and reformation of the nation. It was time to cleanse the land of all pagan influence. It was time to return to the Law of Moses. It was time for God's chosen people to live as God's chosen people and be the living witness to the world that God intended them to be. Instead, Saul became jealous of David and so protective of his power that he lost all perspective. He spent the next few years chasing David around the wilderness trying to kill him.

Are Christian leaders today really discerning when it comes to how God is at work in the world? We need to recognize the people God has chosen—the Davids God has called to fight today's giants. Then we need to work alongside them and turn their victories into movements of God, movements that advance God's Kingdom.

Recently a pastor came to my office and complained about what has become a rather frequent occurrence in the Netherlands: "The Muslims have bought another empty church and are going to convert it into a mosque. Isn't that terrible?"

"No, that isn't terrible," I replied.

"Why not?"

"Terrible is that this church was empty. If the church had been full, there would be no opportunity for a mosque to be there." The time has come for us to understand the real underlying issues we face. The problem is not that Muslims are in my country. The problem is that Christians are like Israel was with the Philistines—weak, disobedient, fearful.

So what did the people of Israel gain from David's victory? For sure that day they regained some dignity. They were no longer the helpless, fearful, intimidated farmers who couldn't even forge a few swords to defend themselves. They enjoyed a great victory, only it was artificial. It was like a football player scoring a great goal and all the fans declaring, "*We* did it. *We* won!"

The fact is Israel didn't do anything to deserve or achieve this win. God did it all through one faithful servant. However, the people could have used this as a chance to learn more about God. They could have returned home to serve heartily the God who promised to protect them if they followed Him and who would abandon them if they didn't.

Did the people really understand the significance of this victory? Or were the echoes of the giant's voice still reverberating in their minds? When Israel returned to their homes and lay down in their beds, did the trauma of those forty days still haunt them? Such brainwashing leaves deep scars. Did Israel really learn the lesson of David's faith?

> FOR REFLECTION: *How do you react to fearful news in your country? It might concern the influx of immigrants or the push to redefine marriage so that men can marry men and women can marry women. Or perhaps it is the latest economic crisis. Does the example of David provide you with any insights into how you might respond?*

34

IT'S NOT OVER YET

*"Then [David] . . . chose five smooth stones from
the brook and put them in his shepherd's pouch"*
(1 Samuel 17:40).

Why did David pick five stones when he needed only one? I believe David was making a prophetic statement. Goliath had four brothers. When David killed Goliath, his brothers would want revenge. David was ready for them. We have to hunt a little in Scripture to find these giants. We will do so in the next couple of devotions and discover some possible significance for us today.

It's important to remember that winning one battle rarely means that the war is over. Someone has said, "Perpetual vigilance is the price of liberty." I can't help but remember how before the end of World War II the churches in Holland were packed. Soon after the Germans departed, the churches emptied. In time the faith of the nation diminished.

We must maintain vigilance as Christians because the spiritual world war will continue until Jesus destroys every rule and authority and power on earth. Jesus must subdue all His enemies. Then He will hand over to the Father *all* the treasures that comprise His Kingdom. You can read this for yourself in 1 Corinthians 15:24–25.

It's worth noting that God didn't call David to fight all the giants. Just one! Once David had demonstrated that giants could be brought down, God allowed others to join the fun. The brutal fact is that these giants had to be annihilated because otherwise they would continue to pose a threat to the first coming of Jesus.

Today the devil continues to try to frustrate the plans of God. He failed to prevent the incarnation. His head was bruised at Calvary (fulfilling Genesis 3:15). Now he seeks revenge against the Church, against the people of God. He is doing all he can to thwart the advance of God's Kingdom.

God uses David as a type of Jesus, the Great Shepherd who defeats the real enemy of us all. In Goliath, the uncircumcised Philistine, we see one type of unbelief. Let's use today's label: atheism. One of the devil's tactics is to try to thwart God's Kingdom. In recent years several books by clever scientists have sought to convince us that there is no God. He is a myth, a figment of our imaginations. We are products of chance and evolution. These "experts" make loud and powerful arguments and gain considerable attention in the media. Sounds like Goliath all over again.

How do we fight the giant of atheism? Our best weapon is faith. It doesn't need to be mature faith. David was just a boy. Despite having little experience in the world, his faith was enough to defeat the atheistic giant. Even at age fifteen or sixteen he was not about to let the uncircumcised Philistine trample the armies of God. Here the teenager was far ahead of the adults in Israel. He saw his countrymen as the army of the living God. However, the army needed to believe this too if they were to be effective.

Without faith you cannot be a real leader, the kind God desires. Have you read recently the list of heroes in Hebrews 11? The list isn't complete. God continues adding to it today. **You can be a champion of faith.** Of course, that will mean suffering and it may cost you your life. That's the reason most people prefer to hide in a crowd—it's safer. You don't have to take risks. Don't stand out; don't be too fanatical. That's where 98 percent of Christians want to live. There are a few who do want to lead but with wrong motives. They want the power that comes with a position. They don't really want to submit their ambition to God's agenda.

You can rise above that. Do you have the guts, by faith in the living God, to step out of the crowd? Remember: **No Guts, No Glory!**

Sure it is dangerous to take on a giant like atheism. It is dangerous to stand up in public for the honor of God whatever the issue. You will become a target. Enemies will shoot at you. Friends may abandon you. That's the risk we take. But that is the war we must fight today. Atheism is just one of the giants we face.

FOR REFLECTION: *If you are to be part of the 2 percent who become champions of the faith, what changes need to take place in you?*

35

WIN THE WAR

"There was war again between the Philistines and Israel" (2 Samuel 21:15).

Victory over Goliath was a landmark triumph for David and Israel, but it wasn't the end and they couldn't rest because their enemy wasn't quitting. War means there are more battles to fight. Oh, if David's victory had been enough to end the Philistine aggression, that would have been wonderful. Unfortunately it wasn't—this war lingered for many years. That's the way it is with spiritual warfare. We can never let down our guard. The devil prowls around seeking whom he may devour (see 1 Peter 5:8).

So Israel and the Philistines must fight again. In 2 Samuel 21 David has been king for some time, and there is war between the Philistines and Israel. David and his men engage the enemy in Gaza, not in Israel—that is progress. David is no longer a young warrior. He doesn't have the energy and strength he once enjoyed and so he grows weary in the battle. Suddenly there is Ishbi-benob, a descendant of the giants. He looms as a threat to the king. Abishai comes to David's aid and kills the giant. After this disaster is averted, David's men tell their leader: "You shall no longer go out with us to battle, lest you quench the lamp of Israel" (v. 17). Here we see hope at work. David set an example for others in Israel to follow, and his faith infused the men around him.

Ishbi-benob had been bent on revenge because David killed his brother. Revenge is a major weapon of our enemy the devil. It has no place in the Christian life or the Kingdom of God. Revenge is what the devil unleashes on those who give valuable service to our Lord Jesus Christ. It is out of this dark domain of revenge that persecution comes.

Over against the reality of persecution, we must have hope. The ministry of Open Doors that God used me to start exists to bring hope to Christians who are threatened or persecuted. The verse that has driven me for decades in serving the Persecuted Church is one of hope: "Wake up, and strengthen what remains and is about to die" (Revelation 3:2).

I wish David's passion had spread to more than just a few of his brave and loyal soldiers. Jesus talked about the little flock. I don't believe we will see a super-sized church in the end times. We will see many little churches, many of them secret communities just barely surviving. That's already the situation today in many countries. These churches must be strengthened. Without hope they will die.

In the next encounter with the Philistine army another giant appears. Saph is his name. Someone else fights him—his name is Sibbecai. This was Sibbecai's moment of glory. He slew Saph. There's not much attention granted Sibbecai, just a brief mention in one verse. All we know about him is that he was from Hushah, a town in the hill country of Judah. His victory is not accorded the attention of David's triumph recorded in 1 Samuel 17. Still it's very important because Sibbecai did his part.

Not all the heroes of the Bible are mentioned by name. But God knows them all. **Will you be faithful to fight your battle regardless of how much, or little, credit you receive?**

FOR REFLECTION: *Who is a hero of the faith you respect today? This may not be a celebrity but someone in your church or community. What do you respect about him or her? What can you learn from this person's example?*

36

THREE DOWN, TWO TO GO

"And there was again war with the Philistines at Gob" (2 Samuel 21:19).

Goliath was back—not the giant David slew, but apparently someone from the same family. He was notable because he had a most intimidating weapon—a spear with a shaft the circumference of a weaver's beam. I don't know how big that is, but it sounds really big. Elhanon stepped up and took this giant down.

By now Israel is tired of fighting giants. Enough! They yearn for peace. Serious battle fatigue has set in. David is off the scene—at least he no longer can lead the troops into battle. Yet the war continues and it must be prosecuted to the very end. Joshua and his armies never did that. They never finished the job. Perseverance is needed until every last giant is killed.

And one more giant remains: "a man of great stature, who had six fingers on each hand, and six toes on each foot" (2 Samuel 21:20). He is not named in 2 Samuel. The hero this time is very interesting. His name is Jonathan and he is David's nephew—the son of Shimei, who happens to be one of David's brothers. What gets Jonathan so riled up that he strikes down this giant? The giant is taunting Israel, probably using the same words as his big brother. Now at least the son of one of those brothers is inspired by David's example. How dare this Philistine insult the people of God! Jonathan took care of this atheist.

Notice that there is nothing original with the insults of these giants. That's because the devil isn't original in his tactics. All he can really do is attempt to paralyze us with his words and size and powerful weapons—to intimidate us and produce fear. The antidote to fear is courage, which Jonathan displays. Finally, the path to the incarnation in Bethlehem is cleared. The devil's giant weapons have been destroyed.

We definitely need more courage today. God supplies the spirit of courage if we believe Him. Paul encouraged his protégé Timothy with these words: "for God gave us a spirit not of fear but of power and love and self-control" (2 Timothy 1:7). We need courage to go after those who defy God and threaten His Kingdom. Many of us, like Timothy, are by nature timid but we won't surrender to the power of the enemy when we apply this antidote to fear and timidity: power and love and self-discipline. The Holy Spirit is ready to provide all of these necessary resources.

The lesson we need to learn from these ongoing battles is perseverance. In the New Testament perseverance is almost always mentioned in connection with official opposition from governments. Jesus tells us that we will be hated for His name's sake, but "the one who endures to the end will be saved" (Matthew 10:22). Jesus is not talking about persevering against sin. He's referring to persecution. They will throw you in prison. That's official. They will kill you—and when family members do the killing, the authorities will look the other way.

There are so many stories from persecuted believers of the beauty of perseverance even in the face of years of imprisonment.

For example, Pastor Allen Yuan in China was imprisoned for twenty-two years for refusing to join the government-controlled church. Listen to the testimony of his wife Alice:

"When my husband, Allen, was sent to prison in April 1958, I was told that I would never see him again. I felt completely miserable and continually blamed God. The future looked so terribly bleak. I had the care of six children and my mother-in-law. I was only earning eighty cents a day. How could I keep my family alive on that? When it all became too much for me, one night I heard a voice: 'My child, I have everything in My hands. These things come from Me.' I replied, 'If these things come from You, please protect me and my family. Do not allow me to dishonor Your name. I want to serve You and glorify Your name.'"

Alice saw God miraculously provide food and other resources for her family. They never missed a meal. One of her trials was that nearly every day the Communist Party required her to report to the police station where they put tremendous pressure on her. "They said that I would never see my husband again, that I should divorce him, and that I should give up my faith. With God's help I kept going. Praying with my eyes closed, I endured the interrogations. After I had been pressured by the security police for six hours, I still had to work for eight hours to earn a living. I had to push handcarts filled with building materials. The carts were much too heavy. I was completely exhausted and was already tired before I started. In the winter, it was even worse. Sometimes I had to shovel cement up onto a floor above my head. The work was dirty, hard, and cold, but I achieved my quota. The others were surprised and wondered where I got the energy from."

Despite all these trials, Alice persevered. When her husband was finally released in 1979, she was able to stand with him, and at age sixty-five, when most people retire, Allen Yuan again took up his vocation as a pastor. Pastor Yuan continued to minister until he was promoted to heaven in 2005 at the age of ninety-one. His wife joined him five years later.

The inspiration of brothers and sisters like Allen and Alice should be enough to motivate us to persevere in service to our Lord and to endure any trials we may face.

All of us have the resources to go after the giants today. We have the Word of God. Our knowledge of the Scriptures, loyalty to our Lord Jesus Christ, and application of God's truths to our lives are all we need. We have more than David had and look what he accomplished. He killed the giant and inspired others to kill giants. We cannot expect others to do what we are not willing to do ourselves. Let's carry on the work God has given us!

FOR REFLECTION: *Are you discouraged or afraid of the unending spiritual battle raging today? What resources can the Spirit of God provide so that you can persevere? (See 2 Timothy 1:7.)*

37

AM I READY TO FIGHT?

"For the weapons of our warfare are not of the flesh but have divine power to destroy strongholds" (2 Corinthians 10:4).

Are you ready to take on the giant God allows in your life? Perhaps you can't know for sure until you confront him. Still there are a few indications that you are ready. You see, the real battle with Goliath took place in David's heart. He learned to know God in the private place where no one could see him—as he took care of the sheep. He listened to the Spirit God placed in him when he was anointed. Therefore he was able to discern the situation as he arrived at the battlefield.

There are three ways we can prove we are fighting the battles God has chosen for us. *First we prove it by our motive.* We do not seek anything for ourselves. We aim for God's glory. There's a famous saying I like that says, "There is no limit to what we can accomplish as long as we don't care who gets the credit." I would amend that. **There is no limit to what we can accomplish when the aim is to make sure *God* gets all the credit.** Do we really seek His glory? If my motive is God's glory and I don't even care about my life, then I can dare to do anything.

Jesus said: "Whoever finds his life will lose it, and whoever loses his life for my sake will find it" (Matthew 10:39). My only motive should be God's glory.

Second, we prove it by our method. We dare not fire the Lord's cannons with the devil's powder. The Apostle Paul says that we don't wage war the way the world does. Our weapons of warfare are not human but divine. We have the resources of Scripture, the Holy Spirit, and the collective power of the Church of Christ to destroy arguments and every lofty opinion raised against the knowledge of God (see 2 Corinthians 10:4–5). We prepare for battle by taking every thought we have captive to obey Christ. Like David, our weapons are testimony and proclamation.

So much of prophecy and teaching today focuses on "my life, my health, my future, my happiness." The devil likes that because his focus is to destroy the Kingdom, and self-centeredness is one of his best weapons. He knows Jesus will win but he wants Jesus to offer a pitiful gift to His Father—just a few souls, not a great harvest. Let's wake up to the devil's strategy! Let's not allow him to keep diverting us from the heart of Jesus. Go, make disciples of all peoples. If each one of us does his or her part, Jesus will present to the Father a powerful and glorious Kingdom.

Finally, we prove a battle is the right one by our faith. This is a faith that compels us to proclaim The Truth. One of my favorite examples is that of Corrie ten Boom when she was speaking in what was then East Germany. She was scheduled to speak in a cathedral and it was packed, with thousands more gathered outside wanting to hear her. This was a Communist country. Preaching was confined to the church building. Not for Corrie it wasn't! She went to see the mayor and said, "I need loud speakers so the crowd outside the cathedral can hear." You can imagine the mayor's reaction. Corrie didn't back down. "You know that Jesus is the Victor, don't you?" she asked, no doubt reminding the man of his Christian roots as a boy.

"Uh yes. I guess."

"Then you know what to do!"

Within an hour there were loud speakers outside the cathedral and half the city heard her preach. That's boldness that emerges from faith, knowing your cause is right. You determine: "I'm going to proclaim The Truth and fight." This was David's example: words followed by action.

Today there is too much talk without action. Well, let's change that. Let's step up and demonstrate our faith to a world that needs to see how powerful our God really is.

We have a tremendous task ahead of us. May God help us gain insight into the giants we must confront. May He give us the skill to proclaim the truth about Him and then the faith to act and see the battle through to the conclusion.

Are you ready? Then go in the power of the Spirit!

FOR REFLECTION: *Whether you are facing a giant right now or will face one in the future, are you prepared? Take a few moments to reflect on your motives, your methods, and your faith.*

38

BACK TO THE FUTURE

"The last enemy to be destroyed is death"
(1 Corinthians 15:26).

Let's go back to the future.

First, go back: Again we ask, what in the world is David doing at the brook? Look closely. He picks up five stones. What does this mean? We are witnessing a prophet speaking not just about the immediate future—killing Goliath and his brothers—I believe he's also pointing to the end of time. He is showing us the faith we should display as we wait for Christ's return.

Now the future: David doesn't look like a prophet. He's not even conscious of the tremendous insight he displays here. No one who is truly used by God is really conscious of his value in the process of unfolding the mighty plan of God. For God will not, under any circumstances, share His glory with puny man. David doesn't want any of the glory. He clearly declares that this is God's battle and God will receive all of the credit. Encouraged by his example, we have the opportunity to display that same faith.

Are you ready to confront giants? Are you inspired by David's example? Then let me suggest the real issue you and I and the worldwide church must face. **The King is coming! He has a program, and you and I have a part to play. Are you ready?**

Now we must be clear. This is Christ's program, not ours. We will not fulfill it, not even by our participation in so-called "world missions" or by strengthening the Persecuted Church. Those things are vital and may help bring back the King, but when the great moment arrives, it will be by His sovereign act. We will be ecstatic and applauding bystanders. We will watch in growing amazement at such *outrageous grace* that allows us, who once were His enemies, to join in this victorious celebration.

In this devotional we have examined the framework in which giants are fought. The back story of the Old Testament is a war in which the devil did everything possible to prevent Jesus from coming. The enemy tried to break through that unbroken line that runs from Paradise to Calvary. Then "Bethlehem" happened—after four hundred years of silence (the time between the Old and New Testaments), years in which neither God nor His prophets spoke. Then light broke through the "silent night." During Jesus' life on earth, Satan's attacks increased as he attempted to derail Jesus from His mission, tempting Him to go it alone apart from His Father, and even trying to kill Him before He reached the cross.

But Jesus *did* reach the cross. He took our sin (of all the world, for all time) upon Himself. Even on the cross He was still challenged: "He saved others," the people mocked; "he cannot save himself" (Matthew 27:42). That was true, but only in the sense that Jesus chose to stay on the cross and finish His redemptive work. Remember David in the field with his sheep. He was willing to die for his sheep. Of course, he didn't die when he fought the lion or the bear or the giant Goliath. But Jesus did. Jesus came to *die* for *sin*, once and for all. And then to rise again three days later, giving us the ultimate victory.

That's where we stand today, with one giant remaining that none of us can slay. Though we may face one or more giants, only Jesus can confront this giant. Paul identifies it in 1 Corinthians 15:26. "The last enemy to be defeated is death." None of us can escape the giant of death. Fear of death has gripped everyone. Trips to the moon or Mars or placing bodies in deep-freeze have not led to any solutions. There is much speculation today that science will extend life and even postpone death indefinitely. I've got news for them. Science will not defeat death.

This giant is huge. But it is the last and final one. Jesus deals with this giant for us. Then finally the war is over: "For God has put all things in subjection under his feet. . . . When all things are subjected to him, then the Son himself will also be subjected to him who put all things in subjection under him, that God may be all in all" (1 Corinthians 15:27–28).

I heard a story once about a man who approached people on the street with the question, "Are you ready to die?" I don't know his motivation but it sure scared people to death. Well, I don't want to scare you. My question to you is this: **Are you ready to live?**

David was full of life when he faced Goliath. It was an adventure. Dangerous? Yes! But exhilarating, too, because if God didn't act, David was doomed. What an exciting way to live!

Remember the picture of David trying to put on Saul's armor? The whole idea was silly. David didn't need *that* armor. He needed spiritual armor. He used what God provided and experienced God's great victory. So in that spirit, I leave you with the most encouraging sentence ever penned in literature: "Therefore take up the whole armor of God, that you may be able to withstand in the evil day, and having done all, to stand firm" (Ephesians 6:13).

Now that's a glorious future! Go and live it!

FOR REFLECTION: *The King is coming! What does that mean to you as you face God's enemy? Inspired by the example of David, how do you respond to the challenge: Are you ready to live?*

NOTES

1 See 2 Samuel 21:16, 18, and 20, and 1 Chronicles 20:4–8.
2 You can read the full story in chapter 6 of *God's Smuggler*, by Brother Andrew with John and Elizabeth Sherrill published by Chosen Books.
3 See *Operation Nineveh: 39 Days with Jonah* by Brother Andrew and Al Janssen, published by Open Doors International.

GET INVOLVED!

Open Doors started in 1955 when a Dutch missionary discovered that Christians in Communist countries were desperately longing for Bibles and supplies—and so he began to take Christian literature behind the Iron Curtain. He became known as Brother Andrew—'God's Smuggler'—and the founder of a ministry still rooted in a passion to follow God's call and release His Word into the lives of believers in the world's most difficult areas.

More than fifty years later Open Doors continues to serve persecuted Christians in around fifty countries, whether the oppression comes in the name of Communism, Buddhism, Hinduism or Islam. Where the people of God are under pressure, Open Doors stands with them, responding to their cries for help and shaping its response under their guidance.

Prayerful involvement with Open Doors is a great way to strengthen the Persecuted Church, not just to face the onslaught of pressure, but to continue to reach out with the Gospel of Jesus Christ.

Right now Open Doors is ready to give you information for your prayers—the authentic voice of the Persecuted Church brought to you in print, by email, and on the web, so that your prayers are timely, informed and effective weapons in the spiritual battle.

Right now Open Doors can channel your gifts to where they will make a significant difference to our sisters and brothers in the Persecuted Church, not least in providing the Bibles and other Christian literature they have requested. You will be helping to train pastors and congregations so that they can stand strong through the storm, to strengthen the Church in its commitment to mission, to make sure that those who have lost so much can receive material help and spiritual encouragement.

Many Christians around the world also volunteer to bring the Persecuted Church into the life of their own church family, sharing news for prayer and exploring the lessons to be learned from our sisters and brothers.

Perhaps you would allow Open Doors to become your link to the Persecuted Church, so that together we can all play our part in God's great plan and purpose for His world. For further information, simply contact the national office listed below—and discover more of the miracles that come in obedience to God's call.

Open Doors AUSTRALIA
PO Box 6237
Frenchs Forest, NSW 2086
Australia
www.opendoors.org.au
Email: ODAustralia@od.org

Open Doors CANADA
8-19 Brownridge Rd.
Halton Hills, ON L7G 0C6
Canada
www.opendoorsca.org
Email: opendoorsca@od.org

Open Doors INDONESIA
ODINDO, P.O. BOX 5019/JKTM
Jakarta 12700
Indonesia
www.opendoorsindonesia.org
Email: indonesia@od.org

ODMAL Services Berhad
PO Box 216
Selangor Darul Ehsan
West Malaysia, 41720 Klang
Malaysia
Email: malaysia@od.org

Open Doors NEW ZEALAND
PO Box 27630
Mt Roskill, Auckland 1440
New Zealand
www.opendoors.org.nz
Email: opendoorsnz@od.org

Open Doors PHILIPPINES
PO Box 1573
Quezon City, QCCPO 1155
Philippines
www.opendoors.ph
Email: philippines@od.org

Open Doors SINGAPORE
Open Doors (S) Company Limited,
8 Sin Ming Road
#02-06 Sin Ming Centre, 575628
Singapore
www.opendoorssg.org
Email: singapore@od.org

Open Doors SOUTH AFRICA
PO Box 1771
Cresta, Gauteng 2118
South Africa
www.opendoors.org.za
Email: southafrica@od.org

Open Doors UK & IRELAND
PO Box 6
Witney
Oxfordshire, OX29 6WG
United Kingdom
www.opendoorsuk.org
Email: inspire@opendoorsuk.org

Open Doors USA
PO Box 27001
Santa Ana, CA 92799
USA
www.opendoorsusa.org
Email: usa@opendoors.org

For information on Open Doors offices worldwide please see **www.OpenDoors.org**.